RUNNING — THE RISK

First published in 1994 by
The Children's Society
Edward Rudolf House
Margery Street
London WC1X 0JL

A catalogue record for this book is available from the British Library.

ISBN 0 907324 93 2

Edited by: Annabel Warburg
Cover design: Beacon Creative

Printed by
The Grange Press
Butts Road, Southwick, Sussex

RUNNING — THE RISK

YOUNG PEOPLE ON THE STREETS OF BRITAIN TODAY

A report based on research
commissioned by The Children's Society
and undertaken by the Child Care Research and
Development Unit,
Department of Adult Continuing Education,
University of Leeds.

Research team and authors:
Mike Stein, University of Leeds
Gwyther Rees, The Children's Society
Nick Frost, University of Leeds

The Children's Society
MAKING LIVES WORTH LIVING

Charity Registration No: 221124

ACKNOWLEDGEMENTS

This study would not have been possible without the active assistance and advice we have received from:

- The streetwork projects: Leeds Safe House, the Porth Project, Safe in the City, Southside and Youth Link.

- The Streetwork Research Group.

- The young people we interviewed or who completed our questionnaire.

- Our colleagues in the Child Care Research and Development Unit and Department of Adult Continuing Education.

- Colleagues from the police, social services and voluntary organisations who assisted with the research.

- Annabel Warburg, Ruth Gardner, Graeme Brown, Keith Drinkwater and Roger Smith for their editorial assistance.

- Caroline Habberley who assisted with interviewing young people.

The authors and The Children's Society are grateful to the New Chasers Charitable Trust for their generous financial support for this publication.

CONTENTS

Page

INTRODUCTION AND BACKGROUND

Chapter 1 – Introduction 3
  'Young runaways'   ·   3
  Origins of The Children's Society's streetwork initiative   4
  Outline of the research   7
  Structure of the report   10
Chapter 2 – Summary of key findings of the research 13

SECTION ONE: THE YOUNG PEOPLE WITH WHOM
THE PROJECTS WORK

Chapter 3 – Description of the young people 19
  Characteristics   19
  Life history   21
  Current situation   28
  Support networks (excluding the streetwork projects)   30
  Behaviour and welfare (apart from running away)   32
  Summary   33
Chapter 4 – 'Running away': young people's perspectives.................35
  First running away incidents   35
  Most recent running away incidents   38
  Young people's running away experiences   40
  Summary   44
Chapter 5 – 'Running away': perspectives of Children's Society
staff and other professionals..45
  Factors leading to young people leaving where they live   45
  Factors leading to young people running from substitute care   47
  Factors relating to all young people   49
  Other issues   50
  Summary   51
Chapter 6 – 'Running away': synthesis of the data.......................53
  Describing the young people with whom the projects work   53
  Sub-groups of young people who run away   56
  A model of running away 'pathways'   61
  Summary   68

SECTION TWO: THE WORK OF THE PROJECTS

Chapter 7 – Models of service provision 71
  Youth Link, Birmingham   71
  Safe in the City, Manchester   72
  Leeds Safe House   74
  The Porth Project, Gwent   76

Chapter 8 - Comparison of the young people in contact with
the projects...81
    Comparison of characteristics and experiences   81
    Comparison of running away experiences   82
Chapter 9 - Outcomes of the projects' work 85
    Catering for young people's immediate needs   85
    Establishing a positive relationship with young people   89
    Facilitating change in young people's situations   90
    Attending to young people's long-term needs   95
    Summary   98
Chapter 10 - Effects of the projects' work...................................99
    Effects on young people   99
    Effects on project staff   102
    Effects on other people and organisations   104
    Summary   105
Chapter 11 - Other issues regarding the projects' work...................107
    Accessibility to young people   107
    Anti-discriminatory issues   107
    A 'young person-centred' approach   109
    Relationships with other agencies   112
    Project development   112
    Summary   114

SECTION THREE: IMPLICATIONS OF THE RESEARCH
FINDINGS

Chapter 12 - A model of intervention 117
    Primary intervention   118
    Secondary intervention   119
    Tertiary intervention   119
Chapter 13 - Social policy issues 121
    The position of young people under 16 living away from both family and
        substitute care   121
    The criminalisation of young people involved in prostitution   122
    The quality of life for young people in substitute care   122
    The level of support provided to young people leaving care   123
    The impact of family breakdown on young people   123
    The potential links between running away and homelessness   124
    Educational issues   124
    The need to develop a co-ordinated response   125
Chapter 14 - Concluding remarks...127

Appendix - Comparison with research in other countries   129
References   132

INTRODUCTION AND BACKGROUND

CHAPTER 1
Introduction

'YOUNG RUNAWAYS'

The Children's Society's work with children and young people living on the streets of Britain dates back to its earliest origins. When Edward Rudolf started the Church of England Central Society for Providing Homes for Waifs and Strays in 1881, he was motivated largely by a concern to 'rescue' the young, homeless 'vagrants' to be found on the streets of Victorian London. One hundred years later, 'young runaways' were still to be found living on the streets of the country's major cities. In response, Edward Rudolf's organisation, now renamed The Children's Society, renewed its work with this vulnerable group of young people. In the 1990s, its 'streetwork initiative' is, in expenditure terms, its second largest programme of work.

Recent research suggests that the issue of young people running away is an important social problem. In 1988, The Children's Society estimated that there were approximately 98,000 incidents of young people under the age of 18 running away from home or substitute care each year (Newman, 1988). Research carried out by the Society in Leeds in 1993 has indicated that as many as one in seven under-16-year-olds run away overnight (Rees, 1993). The research also suggests that around 2% of these young people go on to run away ten times or more. There are currently around 3.5 million young people aged under 16 in the metropolitan counties of England[1]. Thus, if the above figures were repeated amongst this group, we can estimate that 10,000 of these young people would run away ten times or more before their sixteenth birthday.

There is a 'grey area' in the law regarding young people aged 16 and 17 who wish to leave home. Section 20 of the Children Act 1989, for example, states that young people who are experiencing difficulties at home can ask to be accommodated by the local

---

[1] Source: 1991 Census. There are seven metropolitan counties in England: Tyne and Wear, South Yorkshire, West Yorkshire, Greater London, West Midlands, Greater Manchester, and Merseyside.

authorities despite parental objections. In Scotland, young people may leave home at 16 with or without parental consent.

The legal position regarding any under-16-year-old who wants to leave home is that they must apply through formal court proceedings under the Children Act 1989, to substitute parental control with that of another acceptable adult who can take parental responsibility for them. Young people under the age of 16 who have run away from home or substitute care are left in a 'vacuum' as far as statutory support is concerned: they cannot receive welfare benefits; they should be in full-time education; they are legally unable to work; they are not entitled to a Youth Training place; and they cannot enter into contracts to obtain independent accommodation. They therefore have no legal means of supporting themselves.

As this research will show, young people living on the streets of Britain are highly vulnerable, not only to exploitation and danger but also to losing contact with all existing welfare systems and legal means of self-sustainment. Only by examining and attempting to understand the motivations of young people who run away and their experiences, and by evaluating the systems already in place to offer them support, will we be able to identify the most effective ways both of offering alternative solutions to those who want to run away, and of meeting the needs of those who do.

This research examines and evaluates the work of four of The Children's Society's streetwork projects, each of which represent different models of service delivery. The research also explores the situations of the young people they work with, including their backgrounds, the factors that have led them to run away, their own views of their experiences while away from their homes, and their needs and how far these are being met both by the projects and by other support networks. Finally, it offers a model of prevention and early support, together with a series of challenges to all those who have responsibility for children and young people.

ORIGINS OF THE CHILDREN'S SOCIETY'S STREETWORK INITIATIVE

The Children's Society current streetwork initiative has its origins in research undertaken in 1981 into the needs of young homeless people in London. This research identified a glaring gap in provision for young people under the age of 17. By law, voluntary agencies catering for the single homeless could work only with those aged 16 and above. Young people under this age were expected by the law and social convention to live at home with their parents or other carers who had, to use the terms of the 1989 Children Act, 'parental responsibility' for them. Legally speaking then, they could not be 'homeless', but rather 'absent' from home or local authority accommodation. If they ran away and were found by the police, they were normally returned to their homes immediately. For most this gave them little chance to address the problems that had caused them to run in the first place; for many, it meant a return to abusive and violent environments. Many ran again, but tried to make sure they kept well clear of anyone who could return them home.

The need for a safe place for young people to go and get help was clear. The Children's Society responded to this need and in 1985, after four years of extensive planning with other agencies, opened the Central London Teenage Project (CLTP) — the first 'safe house', or refuge, for young runaways in Britain. CLTP offered young people accommodation at a confidential address, a chance to discuss their reasons for running away and their needs, counselling, and help with planning their next move.

In addition, the Society undertook research in an attempt to understand why young people were running away, how many were doing so each year, and how best to respond to the problem. This research and the work of CLTP raised clear national implications: it was not nearly sufficient simply to have a London-based 'safety net'.

A national programme was launched, entitled 'Young People Under Pressure'. Each of the Society's six regions was asked to consider establishing a 'streetwork' project, responsive to locally perceived needs and developed in co-operation with local and national voluntary and statutory organisations. The final result was five projects opening in the late 1980s and early 1990s: these projects were based in Bournemouth, Birmingham, Manchester, Leeds, and Gwent.

The role of the Children Act 1989

When CLTP opened, it faced a serious legal problem. Child care legislation had for many years contained penalties for those 'harbouring' young people under the age of 16 who had run away from family or care settings. This legislation was necessary to prevent exploitation of young people by those wishing to hide them away. However, CLTP refuge was therefore, at least in theory, in breach of the law.

The Children Bill offered a chance to remedy this situation. The Bill was first presented to Parliament in November 1988 and attempted a comprehensive reform of child care legislation. The Bill provided a golden and, perhaps, unique opportunity for The Children's Society to influence Government, and to give the official stamp of approval to the refuge initiative. Yet initially the Bill did not include any clause relating to specified organisations working with runaways. Mobilising its links with its supporters, the Society was able to launch a letter-writing campaign, which resulted in pressures on Members of Parliament to respond to the issue of street children in modern Britain. As a result, the issue was raised and debated at Committee stage and an assurance was given by the Minister that the Government would bring forward an amendment at Report stage.

The final result was Section 51 of the Children Act 1989, which states that:

51. (1)   Where it is proposed to use a voluntary home or regis-
tered children's home to provide a refuge for children who appear to be at risk of harm, the Secretary of State may issue a certificate under this section with respect to that home.

(2)   Where a local authority or voluntary organisation arrange for a foster parent to provide such a refuge, the Secretary of State may issue a certificate under this section with respect to that foster parent.

(5)   Where a certificate is in force with respect to a home, none of the provisions mentioned in subsection (7) shall apply in relation to any person providing refuge for any child in that home.

It is Section 51 that legitimates the existence of the refuge-based projects and ensures that the Society is exempt from the implications of Section 49 of the Children Act and other legislation (Section 71 of the Social Work (Scotland) Act 1968, Secion 32 (3) of the Children and Young Persons Act 1969, Section 2 of the Child Abduction Act 1984). Under Section 49 of the Children Act, it is illegal to keep a child away from a 'responsible person', an offence punishable by imprisonment for a term not exceeding six months, or by a fine. Section 51 is of considerable interest to the student of the Children Act in that at one level it seems to be in contradiction to the concept of 'parental responsibility', perhaps the central concept of the Children Act.

Section 51 is not however the end of the story. It also stipulates that all refuges must be certificated by the Department of Health. In brief, this means that they must meet the stringent standards set down in the two relevant sets of regulations (Refuges (Children's Homes and Foster Placements) Regulations 1991, Children's Homes Regulations 1991). The Regulations allow for a young person to stay in refuge for a maximum of 14 consecutive days, and a maximum of 21 days in any three-month period.

This certification process has not proved to be easy and we discuss the impact of Section 51 in Chapter 11.

OUTLINE OF THE RESEARCH

As we have seen from the above brief history of the streetwork initiative, The Children's Society has been at the forefront of innovative practice in relation to young people who have run away or have been forced to leave where they live. The Society's streetwork programme currently consists of five projects:

Leeds Safe House
Provides a residential refuge and an advocacy service for young people who have run away or have been forced to leave where they live.
Porth Project
Provides a 'dispersed' refuge (with approved foster carers) and an advocacy service for young people in South Wales who have run away or have been forced to leave where they live.
Safe in the City
Works with young people on the streets in Manchester, provides an advocacy service and occasional 'dispersed' refuge.
Southside
Provides refuge for young people in Bournemouth, and runs an advice/information centre.
Youth Link
Works with young people on the streets in Birmingham, runs a drop-in service, and provides an advocacy service.

The innovative nature of the streetwork programme and the consequent opportunities for learning prompted The Children's Society to commission the research described in this report. For a number of practical and historical reasons, the research looked at the work of four of the above projects: Leeds Safe House, the Porth Project, Safe in the City, and Youth Link. This enabled an exploration of the main models of service provision: detached street-based work, drop-in centre work, residential refuge, and dispersed refuge. A more detailed description of the services the projects provide is to be found in Chapter 7. It should also be noted that the Porth Project only began service delivery halfway through the research contract and this has meant that the data we have been able to gather relating to this project is less comprehensive.

The research was carried out for the Society over a two-year period (July 1992 to June 1994) by the Child Care Research and Development Unit at the Department of Adult Continuing Education, University of Leeds. The research director was Mike Stein

(University of Leeds), and the research team was completed by Nick Frost (University of Leeds) and Gwyther Rees (on secondment from The Children's Society).

Research aims and methodology

The main aims of the research were:

1) To clarify the various definitions of 'running away' and, where applicable, the obverse 'keeping in touch'.
2) To investigate the processes and systems leading to young people running away including, where relevant, families and local networks/communities, local authority accommodation (e.g. placements/decision-making), homelessness, income, discrimination on any grounds.
3) To explore the needs of young people who are in contact with the Society, as defined by themselves and other key people.
4) To explore the responses of the projects to young people, including:

- the experiences of project workers in providing a response to young people;
- outreach work, crisis work;
- the different methods, settings and philosophies involved;
- current or proposed changes in the work of the projects and the purpose of these changes.

It was proposed to meet Aim 1 by gathering data in the form of a survey questionnaire from young people using the projects. Aims 2, 3 and 4 were to be met by looking at young people's experience within the projects and after they left the projects, i.e. looking at outcomes. This was to be done by gathering the perceptions of young people, project workers, and other key people.

The research proposal therefore implied the following research methods:

- questionnaires for young people who used the projects;
- interviews with young people who used the projects (with a second follow-up interview where possible);
- interviews with project staff;
- information-gathering from other key people (e.g. social workers).

The final information base gathered through the above methods was:

102 self-completed questionnaires returned by young people;
36 young people interviewed;
49 Children's Society staff interviewed;
28 professionals in other agencies interviewed.

Previous research on running away and street children

In addition to the above information, the research also included a search for UK and international literature on the issues of running away and street children.

The three main previous research studies in the UK have been:

1) Newman, C. *Young Runaways: findings from Britain's first safe house.* The Children's Society, 1988:
   A study of young people at Britain's first refuge for young runaways, plus a nation-wide survey of police missing person statistics.

Key findings:
- incidence of abuse amongst young people who run away;
- over-representation of young people from residential care amongst young people on the streets in London;
- estimated 98,000 missing person incidents (under 18 years old) each year in the UK.

2) Abrahams, C. and Mungall, R. *Runaways: Exploding the Myths.* NCH — Action for Children, 1992:
   A study of police missing person statistics in five areas of England and Scotland.

Key findings:
- estimated 102,000 missing person incidents (under 18 years old) involving 43,000 young people each year in England and Scotland;
- young people generally do not run away to the 'bright lights' but stay in their local area;
- over-representation of young people from residential care amongst young people who are reported missing.

3) Rees, G. *Hidden Truths: young people's experiences of running away.* The Children's Society, 1993:
   A survey of young people in Leeds, plus interviews with young people with recent running away experience.

Key findings:

- estimated 1 in 7 young people in Leeds have run away and stayed away overnight before the age of 16;
- very high incidence of running away amongst young people in residential care, but also a higher incidence of running away from family than had been previously estimated from missing person statistics;
- running away usually starts within the family, even amongst young people who later run away from substitute care.

These studies have therefore all identified significant evidence of young people reported missing, or young people who have run away. All three studies also contained a number of other important findings which are referred to at appropriate places throughout this report.

The international literature research identified 141 articles and books on the issues of running away and street children, most of which were from the USA. Twenty-three of these were obtained, including a comprehensive study by Brennan et al. (1978). A summary of some of the findings of these studies is included in the Appendix.

STRUCTURE OF THE REPORT

A summary of the key findings of the research is found in the next chapter. Following this, the main body of the report is divided into three sections:

Section 1 looks at the young people with whom the streetwork projects work:

Chapter 3 contains a description of the young people's characteristics, life histories, current situations, support networks, behaviour (apart from running away), and welfare.

Chapter 4 looks at the young people's experience of running away or being on the streets.

Chapter 5 examines the perspectives of Children's Society staff and other professionals on the issues of running away and being on the streets.

Chapter 6 concludes Section 1 with a synthesis of the data, a discussion of definitions, and a theoretical model of running away 'pathways'.

Section 2 looks at the work of four of the streetwork projects:

Chapter 7 describes the projects' models of service provision and intended outcomes of their work.

Chapter 8 compares the young people in contact with the four projects.

Chapter 9 examines evidence on the extent to which the projects achieve their intended outcomes with young people.

Chapter 10 considers other potential effects of the projects' work on young people, project staff, and external people and organisations.

Chapter 11 looks at other issues that have arisen in relation to the projects' work, including accessibility, anti-discriminatory issues and processes of working with young people.

Section 3 looks at implications of the research findings:

Chapter 12 considers implications for working with young people who run away or are on the streets, including an integration of preventative strategies into the theoretical model presented in Chapter 6.

Chapter 13 looks at the broader social policy issues raised by the research findings.

Finally, Chapter 14 contains brief concluding remarks on some of the major themes emerging from this research.

CHAPTER 2
Summary of Key Findings of the Research

SECTION 1: THE YOUNG PEOPLE WITH WHOM THE PROJECTS WORK

The young people have generally had a high level of disruption in their lives [Chapter 3].

- Within the family there was a high incidence of relationship breakdown, conflict and violence.
- Most of the young people had spent periods in substitute care and often had had a number of different placements.
- A significant minority of the young people had spent extended continuous periods away from both family and substitute care before the age of 16.
- Amongst the over-16-year-olds, frequent changes of accommodation and periods of homelessness were common.

Most of the young people lacked support networks (apart from the streetwork projects) [Chapter 3].

- There was a high level of detachment from family and (where relevant) social services.
- There was also a high level of detachment from the education system.
- Many young people had a distrust of adults and relied on peers for support.

There were significant levels of substance use, self-harm, depression and criminal offending amongst the young people interviewed [Chapter 3].

- The large majority of the young people had run away before the age of 16 [Chapter 4].
- Most of the young people had first run away from family, usually remaining in their local area, and only staying away for a short time.
- Many of the young people who had run away from family were subsequently placed in substitute care.
- Most of the young people had run away many times and later running away incidents were on the whole more extensive and

13

wide-ranging than first incidents.

- Young people identified a number of positives to being away from where they lived, including relief from pressure and making new friends, but the majority felt that being away had not helped to sort out their problems.
- There were also a number of negative experiences including fear, loneliness, and physical and sexual assaults.
- A majority of the young people had resorted to strategies such as stealing, begging or providing sex for money in order to survive.

Young people's experiences were matched by the perceptions of professionals who worked with them [Chapter 5] and who identified:

- Abuse as a key factor in running away from family.
- Feelings of not being listened to or cared about and bullying as key factors in running from care.
- Economic stresses on parents and resource constraints on local authorities as important contextual factors in understanding running away.

The data gathered has enabled the identification of a number of major pathways in relation to running away from family and substitute care, in some cases leading to 'detachment' from these and other support systems [Chapter 6].

SECTION 2: THE WORK OF THE PROJECTS

The street-based and refuge-based projects all tend to concentrate on working with young people who have already run away a number of times. However, the refuge-based projects often work with young people at an earlier stage of running away experience, while the street-based projects more often work with 'detached' young people [Chapter 8].

The projects aim for four broad outcomes with young people and there is evidence of considerable success in at least three of these areas [Chapter 9]:

- The projects are highly successful at meeting young people's immediate needs. There are some differences in the range of needs met by each of the models.
- The projects have all had significant success in establishing positive relationships with this marginalised group of young people.

- There is also significant evidence of projects facilitating change in young people's lives. There are some differences in the kinds of change achieved by the different models.
- The projects aim to work with young people in the short-term and to engage other agencies in meeting young people's longer-term needs. However, there is considerable evidence that the projects are involved with some young people on a long-term basis.

The research has also highlighted a number of other issues relating to the projects' work, including unanticipated consequences [Chapter 10] and issues of accessibility, anti-discriminatory practice, and processes of working with young people [Chapter 11].

SECTION 3: IMPLICATIONS OF THE FINDINGS

Drawing on the research data, a model of intervention has been developed. This suggests that future work with young people could develop along broader lines [Chapter 12] to incorporate:

- primary prevention (e.g. education in schools);
- secondary prevention (e.g. mediation between parents and young people);
- tertiary prevention (e.g. street-based outreach work and refuge-based work).

There are a number of areas for consideration by other agencies [Chapter 12] including:
- the need for a co-ordinated response to working with young people who run away;
- the need for a response to the issue of young people running from residential care, and in particular to the issue of bullying;
- educational support for this group of young people.

The research has also highlighted a number of social policy issues [Chapter 13], including:
- young people's legal position under the age of 16;
- support for young people leaving care;
- the impact of family breakdown on young people.

SECTION 1

THE YOUNG PEOPLE WITH WHOM
THE PROJECTS WORK

CHAPTER 3
Description of the Young People

In order to obtain a picture of the young people who are in contact with the projects, data was gathered on various aspects of their lives. This data has been grouped into five broad areas: characteristics; life history; current situations; networks; and behaviour and welfare. The information was gathered through self-completed questionnaires (102 people) and in-depth interviews (36 people, 32 of whom were contacted through the projects). In terms of the different projects the young people were in contact with, a distinction is made only where this is important to a full understanding of the data. A detailed comparison of the young people in contact with the projects is to be found in Chapter 8.

CHARACTERISTICS

Age

Exactly half the young people in the questionnaire sample were aged 14 or 15, and the large majority (81%) were under 18:

Figure 3.1 Ages of young people in the questionnaire sample[1]

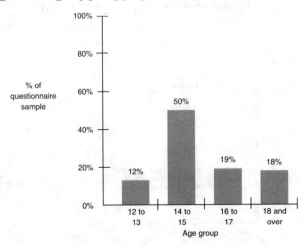

[1] Figures do not add up to 100% due to rounding.

19

Of the interviewees contacted through the projects, 16 people were under 16 years of age and 16 were over 16.

Sex

The questionnaire sample was made up of 59 females and 43 males:

Figure 3.2 *Sex of young people in the questionnaire sample*

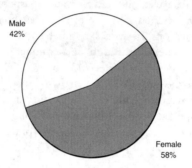

In the interview sample 22 were males and 14 were females.

Origin

The replies to the question on origin were as follows :

Figure 3.3 *Origin of young people in the questionnaire sample*

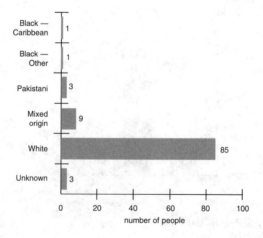

The questionnaire sample size does not permit definitive statements on this issue. It appears that around one in seven of the young people the projects work with are from ethnic minority communities. However, it is important to set this figure within the context of the composition of local populations. The issue of how accessible each project is to young people from all ethnic groups is discussed in Section Two.

Among the interview sample, where known, 31 were white and one person was of mixed origin. This was not unexpected, given the relatively small number of young people from ethnic minority communities using the projects. It should be borne in mind, however, that the research findings may not be applicable to all groups of young people who run away. There remains a need for more focused research into the issue of running away as it relates to young people from different cultural backgrounds (Patel, 1994).

LIFE HISTORY

The interview and questionnaire samples indicate a high level of disruption in most of the young people's lives. Among the questionnaire sample, at least 60% had lived in a family where the birth parents had split up, and around a quarter had lived in a reconstituted family; 70% had lived in substitute care of some form. Of this last group of young people, 84% had lived in a children's home, 57% in foster care, and 17% in a secure unit.

Although the interview data is not from such a representative sample, it gives a more detailed picture of young people's lives[2]. The large majority of young people in this sample had disrupted life histories, characterised by breakdowns in family relationships and periods in substitute care. Most of those contacted through the street-based projects had also spent considerable time 'on the streets' away from both family and substitute care. Of those who were over 16 at the time of interview, very few had a permanent place to live. We deal with each kind of accommodation in turn below.

---

[2] For several reasons it was not possible to gather information from all of the 36 young people interviewed on all the topics below. In some cases the number of people responding on a specific topic has been given in square brackets after the sub-heading. In all other cases the figures relate to 31 of the young people, about whom reasonably comprehensive information was gathered.

Living with family

Family structure

Of 31 young people interviewed, 23 had lived in families where the two birth parents had split up, and in a majority (14) of these cases a new adult (step-parent) had been introduced to the family. Of the remaining eight young people, two had been taken into care soon after birth and adopted or fostered long-term, and a further two had been taken into care by the age of five.

Quality of family relationships[3]

Two of the young people who were taken into care at an early age could not remember anything about the quality of their family relationships. Only five of the other 29 young people spoke positively about any of the family settings in which they had lived. In two of these cases they referred to living with birth parents (although in both cases the young people had left these families and gone into substitute care before the age of ten); the other three cases were adoptive parents, long-term foster care, and a grandparent.

In the remaining 24 cases there were high levels of conflict within the family environment: 16 of these young people spoke of physical violence towards them from one or more parent/step-parent, or in some cases between them and a parent/step-parent. In nine cases this was the male parent/step-parent only; in four cases the female parent/step-parent only; and in three cases both male and female parent/step-parent. The violent incidents were often repeated and extreme. In some cases young people linked the violence with the parent(s) alcohol use, although there is insufficient data to establish a link.

Poor relationships with parents usually went hand in hand with violence for these 16 young people:

> *"My mum married my stepdad. I didn't like him. He battered me a few times and kicked me down the stairs. I still hate him to this day for what he did to me when I was little."*

> *"They [family] always hit me with a belt and marked my back. They hated me."*

---

[3] We include here relationships with adoptive or long-term foster parents for the four young people who had lived in these situations for five years or more.

Recently this young person had thrown a knife at his stepfather during one of many violent fights between them, and had also tried to electrocute him.

Eight young people did not mention physical violence by parents but their comments pointed to a range of other difficulties. The level of emotional disharmony is illustrated by the following quotes:

> "*My favourite part of the family was my dog. That says a lot.*"

> "*They didn't treat me fairly. They wouldn't let me do things, but let the other kids. I've never got on with them since I was five. It felt like I was a lodger.*"

> "*It's very hard to agree with what happened — I was sexually abused* [by stepfather] *when I was little. It was hard to cope with and still is. I was very upset — mum let me down.*"

Substitute care

Types and numbers of placements

Of the 31 young people, 28 had experience of living in substitute care: 26 people had lived in children's homes; over half (17) had lived in foster care; and five had spent time in a secure unit.

Almost half (13 out of 28) of the young people had gone into care after their thirteenth birthday. Consequently, the lengths of time that most had spent in care were relatively short: 16 people had spent less than three years in substitute care.

It was unlikely that all the young people would be able to remember the exact number of placements (in children's homes, foster care or secure units) they had had. However, all but one were able to estimate the number. The average was around five placements per person. These figures are similar to general studies of young people in residential care (Stein and Carey, 1985; Biehal et al., 1992).

The reasons for going into care

Some of the young people, especially those who had gone into care at a young age, were unsure about the reasons why they had gone into care. Eighteen people were able to give their perceptions of the reasons:

- Four people understood the reason to be because they had been abused (either sexually or physically).

- Four people said it was because their parents could not cope. In all four cases this was linked to one of the parents leaving:

  "My mum couldn't cope. Her family rejected her. Her husband left her. She was young. So we came into care."

- Four people said it was due to their parents forcing them to leave home, which meant that they had ended up with nowhere to stay.

- Finally, six of the young people understood it to be because of something they had done:

  "For putting my stepdad in intensive care."

  "I burned down a factory. I got arrested. I thought it was shit."

  "For not going to school. They kept giving me warnings in court but I took no notice, so in the end they took me into care. It was this social worker, she was a bitch. She did everything she could to take me into care."

The experience of living in residential care

Some young people who expressed views about residential care found it "OK". For a few, there was even a sense of relief when they were taken into care, in comparison to their life at home:

  "It was great. It's a different scene. You get food. You don't get hit."

However, there were two recurring themes to young people's feelings about residential care. One sub-group of seven young people expressed ambivalent or indifferent feelings about their relationships with staff and young people in residential care, but complained about the rules, and particularly coming-in times:

  "It was OK. It was better than being at home. Some staff were dickheads. My key worker and some other staff were all right. The other kids were sorted. They had stupid rules. They kept ringing the police. Bed time was 9.30. They were OK with me."

The other main sub-group, also comprising seven young people, expressed strong negative feelings about residential care and mainly commented about bullying by other young people, usually of a severe nature:

> *"There was hardly a day went past when you didn't get hit."* [and in the next placement] *"I got beat up there 'cause I was glue sniffing. I don't mean just bruised. They put me in hospital twice."*

In addition, four of the above young people complained of physical mistreatment or verbal abuse by staff:

> *"The one home was all right until I vandalised it because a member of staff grabbed me by the throat."*

> *"The staff don't do their job properly ... slagging me down, making comments about my weight, like 'You should go on a diet, you're too fat'."*

Another issue that came up for several young people who had lived in care and who identified themselves as gay was a feeling that their sexuality had not been understood by care staff, and their consequent feelings of isolation and lack of support. One young man, for example, felt that his growing awareness of his sexuality whilst in a children's home had not been acknowledged or even "allowed as an option" by the people who looked after him:

> *"They assumed everyone was heterosexual so there was no one I could talk to about it."*

These young people had often been bullied and picked on in care and at school and, in one case, by the male staff in a children's home, for being 'different'.

Finally, it is notable that amongst the two main sub-groups of young people above, six of the seven young people who had been bullied were contacted through the refuge-based projects, whilst all of the seven young people who mainly complained about rules and restrictions were contacted through the street-based projects in Manchester and Birmingham.

The experience of living in foster care

Of the 17 young people who had lived in foster care, some described their foster carers as "all right" but there were also

25

instances of physical mistreatment:

> *"My foster mother tried to suffocate me in my own bed and tried to drown me in the bath."*

whilst some young people felt unwanted:

> *"I didn't like it. They had two children of their own. They treated me and my brother different. They said we were too much trouble."*

Most of the foster placements lasted less than two years and in all but one case young people returned from there to residential care.

The experience of living in secure accommodation

The five people who had been in secure accommodation also had varying feelings about it. Two found it "shit" and "bad"; one felt it was "OK". One young person was positive about the experience:

> *"Good, the best place I've ever been. I had to move on after nine months."*

In at least two cases, the young people felt that they had been placed in secure accommodation because adults had perceived them to be at risk due to sexual activity. In two other cases their placement was the result of having committed criminal offences.

Other places lived before the age of 16

At least seven (four male and three female) of the 31 young people had spent extended periods away from both family and substitute care before the age of 16. They had left at ages ranging from 11 to 15. These young people had spent continuous periods of between six months and three years away and appeared to have relied primarily on friends as a support network while they were away.

It seems remarkable that young people can be adrift from the usual support networks of family or substitute care for such long periods. This group of young people formed one identifiable sub-group of the young people we interviewed. Some of the main details of their situations are presented in the table below:

Table 3.4 Young people who had spent extended periods away

Sex	Age left	Where left	Length of (continuous) time away before 16	Where stayed
Male	14	Foster care	2 years	Always at friends
Female	12	Residential care	2 years	Hotels (paid), old empty flats, rough on the streets
Male	14	Residential care	6 months	Girlfriend's flat
Female	13	Family	1 year	"Here, there and everywhere"
Male	14	Family	2 years	Friend's and all-night venues
Female	11	Family	3 years	Most nights in town, weekends at stepfather's
Male	13	Family	3 years	On the streets and with friends

Places lived after the age of 16

Sixteen of the 31 young people were over 16 years of age at the time of the interview. Most of these young people had lived in several places since their sixteenth birthday. With one exception they had all left family or substitute care permanently. Six had spent time on the streets, nine had been in a hostel, four had had their own flat, and four had lived with friends. Hostels were generally unpopular, and those who had lived in them complained about the standard of accommodation and, above all, about the rules:

> *"I wouldn't advise it. It's packed with drugs and crime. I left because I'm not into drugs and I'm certainly not going to break the law."*

> *"It's shit food and you get kicked out from 12.30 to 5.30."*

> *"I don't like hostels much. I can't stand being in a place where the rules are too strict. It really does my head in."*

Consequently most of the stays in hostels by the young people interviewed had been short, and some had opted for living on the streets instead.

CURRENT SITUATION

The picture amongst the over-16-year-olds is quite different from that amongst the under-16-year-olds, for the legal reasons outlined in the introduction.

People aged under 16

Questionnaire sample:

One of the questions on the questionnaire asked young people to classify their current situation:

> I've run away from where I live
> I've been forced to leave where I live
> I've got somewhere to live
> Other (please describe)

Of the 61 young people under 16 in the questionnaire sample, 48 described themselves as having run away. Of these, 29 had run away from family, 15 from residential care, and four from other places.

A further seven young people described themselves as having been forced to leave where they lived, four from family, two from residential care, and one from foster care.

Most of these young people who had run away or been forced to leave (42 out of 55) were in refuge at the time they completed the questionnaire. Seven of the remainder were staying with friends or relatives and three were sleeping rough. (In three cases, there was no response to this question.)

The other six under-16-year-olds described themselves as having somewhere to live: four were currently staying with friends.

Figure 3.5 The situation of young people under 16 at the time of completing the questionnaire

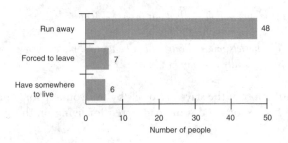

Figure 3.6 Where young people under 16 had run from (current occasion)

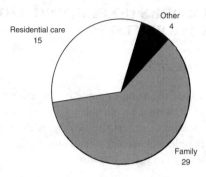

Interview sample:

In the interview sample, also, the majority of under-16-year-olds (13 out of 16) described themselves either as having run away or as having been 'kicked out' by family. Six of these young people were in refuge, six were staying with friends, and one had nowhere to stay. (The remaining three young people had not currently run away.)

People aged 16 and over

Questionnaire sample:

In the questionnaire sample there were 37 young people aged 16 and over. Seven of these people described themselves as having run away, and a further seven as having been forced to leave where they lived. Four of these young people had last lived with family, three in residential care, three in their own place, and four in other places.

The other 23 young people did not classify themselves as having run away or been forced to leave where they lived. Of these, nineteen had somewhere settled to live: at least nine had their own place; at least six were living with family or friends; and two were living in a hostel. The remaining four young people were either living on the streets, or temporarily living with family or friends.

Interview sample:

The over-16s in the interview sample were in a similar variety of situations, including homelessness, staying with friends or relatives, or living in their own accommodation. Few of these young people described themselves as having currently 'run away'.

None of the over-16s interviewed had a paid job.

SUPPORT NETWORKS (EXCLUDING THE STREETWORK PROJECTS)

Family

Around two-thirds (20) of the young people in the interview sample were currently in contact with a parent. However, in some cases this contact was infrequent, and in others the quality of the regular contact was poor. For example, one young person aged 15 described her current relationship with her family as follows:

> "I saw my mother two months ago. She has said she doesn't want to have anything to do with me any more. She's trying to get her own back on me. I went to stay with my dad [recently] but he kicked me out for smoking. He's strict."

In fact, only six of the 31 people had regular and positive contacts with a parent, and a further four had positive contacts with another family member (sibling, aunt/uncle, or grandparent).

Field social workers

Nineteen people out of the 30 who responded on this topic were currently in touch with their social worker, although only nine had regular contact. Interviewees were asked to respond to five statements about their current or last social worker, and the responses from 18 people were as follows:

Table 3.7 Interviewed young people's responses about social workers

	Yes	Some-times	No
1. She/he takes what I say seriously	7	3	8
2. She/he does things behind my back	10	1	7
3. She/he ignores what I tell them	9	3	6
4. If I have a problem, I feel I can talk to her/him about it	3	3	12
5. She/he lets me make my own decisions	6	5	7

The overwhelmingly negative response to statement 4 highlights the importance of the issue of trust, which came up in a number of young people's comments:

"He wasn't too bad — used to say things as they were — didn't hide anything. I liked that about him."

"If you tell them something they'll go and repeat it back to your mother."

The above table does not, however, indicate the distribution of individual feelings across the five statements. As a rough guide for the purpose of summarising the data, if a positive answer is scored as +1, a mixed answer as 0, and a negative answer as -1, the distribution of ratings was as follows:

Figure 3.8 Distribution of young people's responses about social workers

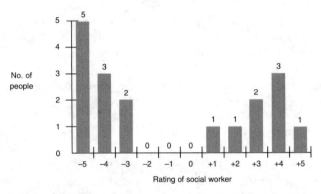

Thus feelings were polarised, with ten people feeling predominantly negative about their social workers, and eight feeling fairly positive with some reservations. However, these responses do need to be considered within the context of the roles and responsibilities which social workers have, as we discuss in Chapter 9.

Residential social workers

A similar scale to that employed for field social workers above was also used for residential care staff. However, with fewer young people responding to these statements, we cannot produce comparisons with the above table. Young people's feelings about residential care staff were mixed. In particular, there were a number of examples of positive feelings about key workers, although this sometimes went hand in hand with feelings of poor relationships with other members of staff (see, for example, the quote on page 25). Again, we need to view this issue within the context of the roles which residential care staff have to fulfil.

Education [23 respondents]

Only four of those in the interview sample who responded on this topic were still regularly attending school or another educational establishment. Suspensions and expulsions were common, and amongst the under-16s in the questionnaire sample, some considered they had left school permanently at as young as 13 years of age.

> *"I did say I would go back, but then the school said it wasn't worth it 'cause I'd been away for so long."* (15-year-old)

Some people linked their detachment from school with going into care:

> *"It's changed a lot since I've been in homes. I used to be good at school work and attendance. But since I've been in homes a lot of things have happened and you don't care and you feel other people don't care."*

Amongst the over-16-year-olds, only one person had any GCSE passes.

Other agencies [30 respondents]

Only a minority (11) of the young people had contact with other agencies: day centres (four); solicitors and/or probation officers (four); counsellor (one); health visitor (one); and psychiatric service (one).

Friends

As noted above, a number of the young people interviewed at the street-based projects were currently living with friends, who appeared to be a relatively major network of support.

BEHAVIOUR AND WELFARE (APART FROM RUNNING AWAY)

Self-harm [24 respondents]

Eleven young people (six males and five females) in the interview sample had tried to harm themselves in the previous three months. This involved either slitting their wrists, overdosing, or attempting to hang or strangle themselves:

"I tried to strangle myself because I was sick and tired of the bullying [by young people in a children's home] *so I wanted to end it for them."*

Substance use [24 respondents]

Fifteen young people used drugs (predominantly cannabis and amphetamines) and six (including two drug users) used solvents or other substances:

"I still have panic attacks from all the drugs I took — mostly acid, some speed, heroin in spliffs. I used to sell about 30 tabs a day and I'd be taking three a day myself."

However, only four of the solvent users and two of the drug users felt that their usage was a problem. One of these young people also felt they had a problem with alcohol use.

Criminal offending [24 respondents]

Sixteen people (nine males and seven females) were currently or had recently been in trouble with the police. The most common offences were property offences (burglary, stealing cars, shoplifting), but at least four of the young people (three males and one female) had warrants out for violent offences (grievous bodily harm, wounding someone, etc.). It was quite common for the young people interviewed to be being pursued by other people they had become involved with whilst on the streets. Often this was related to offending:

"There's a big geezer after me. Last time I saw him he threw me into a shop window. I was selling acid and he didn't like it."

Depression [23 respondents]

There was a high incidence of self-reported depression amongst the interview sample: five young people said they had been depressed most of the time during the last three months, and a further ten some of the time. The high level of self-harm reported above is further evidence of many of the young people's mental states.

SUMMARY

The young people with whom the projects work have usually had highly disrupted lives, characterised by fragmented and often violent family environments, and periods in substitute care.

The majority of under-16-year-olds contributing to the research were living away from their 'official' accommodation. Some had been away for lengthy periods stretching to months or years. Amongst the over-16s, frequent changes in accommodation and periods of homelessness were common.

Most people had only limited links with other adults (excluding the streetwork projects), and had either poor or no contact with family and with social services. Friends were a key element of their support networks. Many under-16s had lost contact with the education system, and amongst the over-16s formal education qualifications were rare. None of the over-16s interviewed had a paid job.

Self-harm, depression, substance use, and involvement in criminal offending were all common aspects of the young people's lives.

Despite the short-term benefits of running away (see Chapter 4) and the relief from the situations that have triggered the decision to leave, the consequences for many are an increasing isolation from all the usual support systems available to young people.

CHAPTER 4
'Running Away': Young People's Perspectives

'Running away' is a far from satisfactory term to describe the wide variety of situations described in this report. This is discussed more fully in Chapter 6, but in the meantime we shall continue to use the term as a convenient shorthand to describe any situation where a young person under the age of 16 chooses or is forced to leave their usual accommodation (either family or substitute care) and stays away for at least one night.

The vast majority of young people in both the interview sample and in the questionnaire sample (94% and 88% respectively) had run away at least once before the age of 16. The two methods of data collection enable different aspects of young people's running away experiences to be explored.

FIRST RUNNING AWAY INCIDENTS

Age and place first run from

A large majority (88%) of young people in the questionnaire sample had first run away from family. Seven per cent had first run from residential care and 5% from foster care. One-quarter (24%) had run away before the age of 11.

Figure 4.1 Where people had first run away from (questionnaire sample)

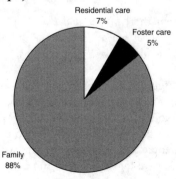

Residential care
7%

Foster care
5%

Family
88%

Figure 4.2 Age at which people had first run away under 16 (questionnaire sample)

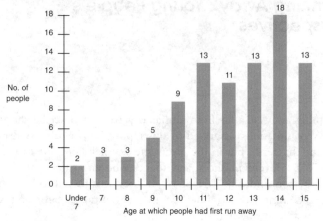

In the interview sample, 28 young people were able to remember the first time they ran away. Again, the large majority (22) of the young people had first run from birth or adoptive families at ages ranging from six to 15. The others had either first run from residential care (four) or from foster care (two).

Factors leading to young people running away

Considering the family backgrounds of the young people in the interview sample, described in the previous chapter, it is not surprising that violence appeared as a common factor leading up to many first running away incidents from family:

> *"Because of my stepmum hitting me and she were trying to get my family split up. She kicked one of my brothers out and my other brother were in care since he were 13."*

> *"Because dad [stepfather] hit me and broke my cheekbone and jaw. The school got the social services. My mother asked me to go as dad would have carried on hitting me."*

Other factors were arguments or not getting on with parents or step-parents, parents drinking, and differential treatment of siblings.

The numbers of young people who first ran from substitute care are too small for it to be possible to identify common themes, but bullying by young people and poor relationships with staff were both reasons young people gave for deciding to run away. For example:

"They just wouldn't move me [change of residential placement]. *The staff didn't do their job proper."*

"To get back at the staff."

Time spent away from family or substitute care

Most first running away incidents of young people interviewed were of short duration (under three days) and it was common for young people either to sleep rough locally or to go to friends or relatives for help:

"I ran away because mum hit me [at ten years of age]. ... *I slept in a shed. I was away for four days. I was on my own. The police took me back. Me mum didn't say anything."*

"I stayed at my cousin's for two nights. My cousin rang ChildLine but that was no good. When I went back to my cousin's [after going out] *my mum was there looking for me and took me back and she was being really sarcastic. She used to send me up to the bedroom and tell me to stay there all night ... and she came up, I was lying on my bed and she started hitting me so I just pushed her out of the way and hit her to stop her hitting me. And that's when I got up and left the house. I ran off to my cousin's again and told them what happened ... Then my sister came and me being stupid I left with her and we spent the night homeless. The next day I came up here* [streetwork project] *and by the end of the day they had me in a children's home."*

The sequence of events illustrated in this last quote is also evident for other young people:

"I'd had enough of my parents. I left home and went round to a friend's. They rang the social services. They contacted the police and I was taken into care. I was upset but it was OK once I got there. I missed my family and I was stupid enough to go back home." (young person aged 14)

At least one-third of the young people had had contact with the police the first time they ran away. Sometimes the police returned the young person home and on other occasions the police initiated the involvement of social services.

Links between first running away incidents and going into care

The last two quotes above illustrate the potential link between starting to run away and the process of being taken into care. This link is confirmed by data from the interviews and questionnaires.

In the interview sample, of the 22 people who had first run from birth or adoptive family, 19 subsequently lived in substitute care. Of these, 14 had permanently left their family and moved into substitute care within about a year of first running away.

In the questionnaire sample, of the young people who had lived in substitute care and had first run from family, two-thirds (65%) had last lived with family at the same age as they first ran away, and a further 13% at only a year older.

MOST RECENT RUNNING AWAY INCIDENTS

Places run from

Around three-fifths (61%) of the questionnaire sample had most recently run from their family, and just over a quarter (27%) from residential care. The remaining 12% had run from various other temporary places of accommodation.

Factors leading to young people running away

Under a quarter of the questionnaire sample had planned to run away, which suggests that most running away happens on the spur of the moment, although there was a high rate of non-response to this interview question.

A list of factors was drawn up from previous research into running away (see Chapter 6), and the questionnaire asked young people to indicate which had happened before they ran away on the most recent occasion. The responses are presented below (some people answered 'Yes' to several factors):

Table 4.3 Factors leading to young people running away

	Total	Family	Resid-ential care	Foster care	Other
People didn't listen to you	39	24	10	2	3
Somebody was violent towards you	38	29	7	1	1
People didn't care about you	29	19	6	2	2
Somebody was bullying you	16	5	8	1	2
Trouble at school	13	9	2	1	1
Somebody drank too much alcohol	9	9	0	0	0
Somebody sexually abused you	6	4	1	1	0
Somebody asked you to run away	4	1	1	2	0
Somebody didn't like you being gay/lesbian	3	3	0	0	0
Somebody was racist to you	2	1	0	0	1
Number of people	**81**	**51**	**22**	**4**	**4**

These figures provide further evidence of the high incidence of violence within the family (29 out of 51 people). The other two most common factors in the family were feelings of not being cared about and not being listened to. For young people in residential care, the four most common factors were feeling that people did not listen, or did not care, being bullied, and suffering violence.

Thirteen of the 16 young people aged under 16 in the interview sample had currently run away, ten from residential care and three from family. The reasons given by some young people for running away from residential care reflect young people's experiences of living in care described in the previous chapter:

> *"The staff lost control over the kids and there was nothing they could do. They were very short staffed. I was physically bullied all the time. I couldn't even go to bed without getting my head kicked in."*

> *"I didn't like the way they treated me — stopping pocket money and threatening to chuck me out."*

Others seemed to have developed a pattern of being away from care, and it was more a question of why they should go back there, rather than why they ran away:

> *"Sometimes I go back if I need a bed or the coppers pick me up."*

The young people currently running from their family gave similar reasons to those which have already been discussed above, including power struggles with parents, and being forced to leave:

> *"My mother wrecked my social life then she wrecked my love life and now after 15 years of pure hell I have finally escaped. There are more reasons as to why I left and many people will probably think they are 'normal' and happen to every family but it gets to a point where you just can't take any more shit and you have to get out before you go crazy."*

> *"My dad kicked me out. Well, in a way he kicked me out, in a way I ran away. He says, 'When I get home from work, I'm going to get you in a car and leave you on her [mother's] doorstep and see what she can do'."*

Time spent away from family or substitute care

Two-fifths of the young people in the questionnaire sample had spent more than a week away, and over two-thirds had sought help or advice, mainly from friends (28) and the street work projects (27). Amongst the interview sample, seven young people had spent long periods away, as outlined on pages 26 - 27.

YOUNG PEOPLE'S RUNNING AWAY EXPERIENCES

The questionnaire sample provided valuable information about young people's running away experiences, including how often they had run away, where they went, positive and negative aspects, and the survival strategies they used.

Number of times run away

More than a third of the questionnaire sample had run away ten times or more:

Figure 4.4 Number of times young people in the questionnaire sample had run away

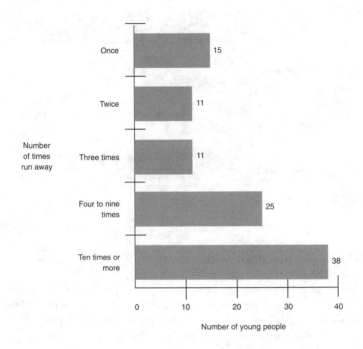

Number of times run away

Once	15
Twice	11
Three times	11
Four to nine times	25
Ten times or more	38

Number of young people

Where people had gone

More than two-thirds of the questionnaire sample had gone outside their local area on at least one occasion. People's destinations were diverse, and included neighbouring towns, seaside towns, and large cities such as Birmingham, Manchester and London. It was possible to categorise 73 of the 90 replies as follows:

• people who had never been out of their local area (the town/ city they came from);
• people who had been outside their local area but not outside their region (Yorkshire, Lancashire, West Midlands, Gwent for the four projects);
• people who had been outside the region but had not gone to a big city;
• people who had gone to a big city outside their region (Birmingham, Dublin, Leeds, Manchester or London).

41

Figure 4.5 Where young people in the questionnaire sample had run to

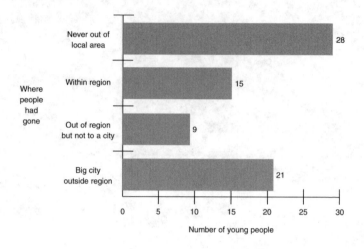

Where people slept while away

Almost two-thirds of the questionnaire sample had slept 'rough' while away, but as previous research has indicated (e.g. Rees, 1993), this should not be equated with traditional images of sleeping in city centres in shop doorways. Whilst a minority did this, the majority of young people we interviewed were extremely resourceful in finding places to sleep for the night. Examples include derelict buildings, garages and outhouses, stairways to blocks of flats, hospital waiting rooms, railway carriages, parks, cemeteries, and out in the country.

Feelings about running away

Young people were asked a number of questions about their feelings about running away. Their responses are shown below.

Table 4.6 Positive aspects of running away

	Yes
Did it give you time to think?	79%
Did you make friends?	79%
Did it give you relief from pressure?	75%
Were you happier than before?	57%
Did you have a good time?	53%
Did it help sort out your problems?	32%

There appear to have been a number of short-term benefits of running away.

> "I didn't have to put up with my mum verbally abusing me and drinking and I didn't have to argue."

In response to an open question about the good things about running away, many young people emphasised the feeling of freedom which it gave them.

> "I had freedom, was allowed to do what I felt I wanted to do."

However, fewer than one-third of young people felt that it had helped them to sort out their problems.

> "My advice to people is try to sort out your problems because running away just makes them worse."

The negative aspects of running away were considerable and illustrate how frightening the experience can be:

Table 4.7 Negative aspects of running away

	Yes
Did you feel hungry/thirsty?	58%
Were you frightened?	43%
Did you feel lonely?	38%
Were you ill?	36%
Were you physically hurt?	26%
Were you sexually assaulted?	11%

As one young person said:

> "It's very scary and no one wants to be near you. You smell and become a liar and you're very lonely."

Many of the young people gave graphic examples of the kinds of risks they face whilst away from family or substitute care:

> "Nowhere to sleep, no food, have to shoplift, being cold. You get into a lot of trouble if you're not careful."

> "Many times I was approached by men who invited me home with them." (young male)

43

Survival strategies

Over half (56%) of the questionnaire sample had stolen or shoplifted while they were away, and at least one in seven (15%) had provided sex for money. Amongst the interview sample, the majority of young people had resorted either to stealing, begging, or sex for money to sustain themselves while they were away:

> *"Committing offences — getting £10 to £30. Theft from a meter, motor vehicle, street robbery. You couldn't stay at one thing too often because the police would catch you. I tried begging but it's embarrassing."*

> *"I had no money, I was upset constantly. I was in bad health and I became a thief and a prostitute."*

> *"The first night I got here I started talking to a few blokes up town. They were on the game. It's the only way I managed to survive — four years constantly every night."*

SUMMARY

The findings presented in this chapter are consistent with previous research on running away in the UK. Early running away incidents are predominantly from the family home, are often very brief, and almost all occur before the age of 16. Violence is an important factor in many young people's decisions to start running away.

As a result of running away, attention is often drawn to the family situation and this can lead to the young person being removed from the family and placed in substitute care. Once in care, many young people continue to run away.

Many young people who run away find themselves in risky situations with nowhere safe to spend the night. Thus whilst running away can offer a respite from stressful or abusive home situations, it often leads to a new set of dangers. Lack of money often leads young people to desperate means to survive on the streets.

It is clear that there is a great deal of diversity in running away incidents and there are some suggestions in the above data that early running away incidents tend to be different in character from later ones. This is discussed more fully in Chapter 6.

CHAPTER 5

'Running Away': Perspectives of Children's Society Staff and Other Professionals

During the interviews with Children's Society staff and professionals in other agencies who have contact with the projects, we sought perspectives and knowledge on the issues of young people being away from where they lived. Apart from being valuable in themselves, these perspectives provide a body of information which can be compared and contrasted with the data gathered from young people described in the previous chapter.

FACTORS LEADING TO YOUNG PEOPLE LEAVING WHERE THEY LIVE

In all, 47 of the adults interviewed (34 Children's Society staff and 13 professionals from other agencies) commented on their perceptions of the factors leading to young people leaving where they live, and most made a distinction between young people living with family and young people living in substitute care. There were many similarities in the perceptions of the factors. But there were also some key differences.

Factors leading to young people leaving family

Twenty-one staff and ten professionals from other agencies commented on this specific area. The factors fell into the following categories:

(a) Abuse and neglect (15 staff and six external professionals):

Generally people made a distinction here between three sub-categories: physical; sexual; and emotional/psychological abuse. Emotional abuse, however, spills over into some of the other categories below and was recognised as being the most difficult to define.

(b) Breakdowns in family relationships (13 staff and four external professionals):

Most of the comments in this category related specifically to relationship breakdowns between parents and/or the introduction of a step-parent figure.

> *"Often marital breakdown ... young people don't feel they belong any-where — each parent has a new partner."* (external professional)

> *"Competition with siblings and/or step-parents or new partner of parent. I think reconstituted families are a major issue."* (project worker)

(c) Lack of support, care or parenting (seven staff and two external professionals):

Included in this category are feelings of not being listened to, development being thwarted, and parents being unable to provide support to their children:

> *"A chain of children born to adults who, because of their own emotional/physical/spiritual deprivation as children, are unable to provide emotionally for the children in their care."* (project worker)

(d) Power struggles — parents not allowing young people to grow up (seven staff and two external professionals):

The two linked themes here were over-strict discipline and a tendency not to recognise the child as developing into a young adult:

> *" ... arguments over boundaries and rules — growth towards adulthood. Young people push boundaries and they get slapped down..."* (project worker)

(e) Generally poor family relationships (five staff and two external professionals):

There were non-specific comments on issues such as arguments and lack of communication between parents and children.

(f) Economic factors (two staff and five external professionals):

It is perhaps significant that this category was mentioned more often by external professionals, most of whom were social workers who would have more contact with parents than would project staff. Economic stresses on parents were seen as having a follow-on impact on children, which could lead to young people being thrown out of home.

(g) Other factors:

A variety of other factors were mentioned by project staff. Two people mentioned inappropriate levels of responsibility being placed on young people. Other factors mentioned by one person were pressure from siblings, differential treatment of siblings, peer pressure drawing the young person out of the home and alienating them from parents, and running away for fear of a parent finding out something that the young person had done.

FACTORS LEADING TO YOUNG PEOPLE RUNNING FROM SUBSTITUTE CARE

Eighteen staff and ten professionals from other agencies made comments on this area. The large majority of comments related to residential care only. The main categories were:

(a) The care system not meeting young people's needs (11 staff and seven external professionals):

The care system was seen by many people as failing to meet some young people's needs and thus leading them to run away from or leave their placements. Some factors were seen as being linked to the shortage of resources currently available to the care system:

> " ... *children's homes' resources are poor, and lack of training means that young people's needs are not being met.*" (external professional — social services)

In other cases, the provision of care in a children's home setting was seen as inherently problematic:

> "*The care system is by its very nature abusive — the separation of the responsibility of a parent and being in control, changing of shifts, etc. — regardless of the quality of care provided.*" (external professional — social services)

There were also gaps between specific young people's needs due to their experiences before coming into care, and the subsequent care provided to them:

> "*There are certain young people who the department can't meet the needs of ... young people who are so severely traumatised that they can't survive*

47

in a situation like a children's home, there's not enough staff and they get bullied." (external professional — social services)

There are great difficulties in providing care to some young people who end up in the care system, either in residential care or foster care:

"She's had a lot of rejections in the past and now she wants to reject them before they reject her. The damage was done before she came into care, some of her experiences in care haven't helped." (external professional — social services)

(b) Not being listened to *(nine staff):*

The feeling that young people were not listened to was a common theme amongst staff within the streetwork projects and it is interesting that it was not mentioned by any external professionals. This is perhaps more a matter of a different use of language, however, as there were examples amongst professionals of similar ideas:

"They feel that there is no other solution available to them: no one to talk to about it; no one to mediate." (external professional)

(c) Bullying by young people *(six staff and three external professionals):*

Both project staff and external professionals reported examples of bullying by other young people.

(d) Mistreatment by residential care staff *(five staff):*

Again, this was a factor mentioned only by staff within the projects. References were made to young people being picked on or bullied by residential care staff, although some stated that they felt it was only applicable in a minority of cases.

(e) Power issues *(four staff and two external professionals):*

This was similar to the corresponding category for young people leaving their family. People felt that decisions (e.g. about placements) were often made without consulting young people, and this led to young people 'voting with their feet'. In some cases it was not that power was being used inappropriately, but that it did not correspond to young people's previous experiences:

"Some young people are facing control and discipline for the first time in children's homes." (external professional — social services)

FACTORS RELATING TO ALL YOUNG PEOPLE

Some factors leading to 'running away' applied to all young people, whether they had been living with their family or in substitute care.

(a) 'Pull' factors (three staff and one external professional):

There were attractions for some young people in spending time away from where they lived and, in particular, going to city centres:

"The street is an exciting place to be." (project worker)

"Young women being attracted to the city centre by money. Whatever they're doing they're being paid for their services." (external professional)

(b) Issues regarding sexual identity (two staff and one external professional):

For some young gay people living with family or in substitute care, their growing awareness of their sexuality is met by a hostile reaction from the people they live with (family, care staff, peers) and from their friends.

(c) General lack of love and care (three staff):

"A lot [of young people on the streets] *tell you that they lack love and care and feel abandoned."* (project worker)

(d) Detachment from society (six staff):

Some staff responded in broad terms to the questions about the causes of young people leaving where they live. A theme here was that some young people cannot fit into the traditional and accepted patterns of growing up and, as a consequence, become detached from mainstream society:

"I think we're talking about the way in which society deals with so-called 'problem behaviour' of young people. We have legitimised routes to growing up which are very restrictive. Some young people don't fit into these and often find 'illegitimate' routes." (manager)

(e) Other factors:

One project worker mentioned problems at school as a factor that can lead young people to leave where they live. Another mentioned young men trying to escape from other young men who were pursuing them. Several project workers mentioned factors which are strictly only relevant to over-16-year-olds, e.g. leaving the care system without adequate preparation resulting in homelessness, and young women fleeing violent boyfriends with whom they were living. This overlap between the issues of running away or spending time on the streets, and youth homelessness, points to a problem with definitions which we discuss in detail in Chapter 6.

OTHER ISSUES

Two other important issues relating to young people away from where they live were raised by several people.

Young people involved in prostitution

This was a significant issue mentioned by a number of people in different cities. Project staff and external professionals were aware of young women and men who were involved in prostitution whilst they were away from where they usually lived:

> *"It's been a revelation for me to know how active town is in terms of prostitution. Some young men use it as a means to an end. At the other end of the spectrum there are those who are abused by it and lack the power to get out of it … Most of the youngsters working in the 'rent scene' are doing it as a way of making a living."* (project worker)

Development of patterns of being away

Some workers commented on the way in which time spent away from family or substitute care develops into a pattern of increasing estrangement and detachment:

> *"Our experience is that they have had a career of estrangement, becoming increasingly detached from meaningful social networks. Difficulties in the family lead to contact with statutory agencies. They become separated from family relationships. Then in substitute care, their needs are not met. They become detached and end up in the city centre community."* (manager)

> *"The causation is a breakdown of communication and a feeling that no one cares, or at the extreme as a result of abuse. Initially young people might not go very far, but then they move away, pulled onto the street. The new sub-culture gives a thrill ... the street becomes a pull, it replaces the needs the young people cannot get in mainstream society. It becomes a positive."* (manager)

We return to this theme in the next chapter, where we consider the evidence for the concept of running away 'pathways'.

SUMMARY

The opinions of Children's Society staff and other professionals who have contact with the projects as to the factors that lead to young people leaving family or substitute care correspond closely to the information gathered from young people presented in the previous chapter.

For young people leaving family, the two most important contributory factors put forward by professionals were abuse and relationship breakdowns, both of which come across strongly in young people's own accounts of leaving home.

For young people in substitute care, the most common factors suggested by adults were young people's needs not being met, young people not being listened to, and bullying. Again, this covers the most common factors given by young people.

Three major themes sum up more than two-thirds of the comments made by Children's Society staff and other professionals. All of them focus specifically on the relationship between young people and their carers:

1. Poor relationships between carers and young people:

- the results of parental relationship breakdown (family)
- generally poor relationships (family)
- young people not being listened to (substitute care).

2. Lack of care and support for young people:

- lack of support, care and parenting (family)
- the care system not meeting young people's needs (substitute care)
- general lack of love and care (family and substitute care).

3. Nature of power relationships between carers and young people:

This theme covers a range of factors, from over-exertion of discipline by carers from the young person's point of view, to perceived abuse of the carer's position of power over the young person in the form of physical, sexual or emotional abuse:

- abuse and neglect (family)
- parents not allowing young people to grow up (family)
- power issues (substitute care)
- mistreatment by staff (substitute care).

From the experience of professionals in contact with young people, therefore, the major explanatory factor for young people leaving family or substitute care is a difficulty in their relationships with their carers, which often fall short of the level of support and care which the young person wants or needs.

The comments of professionals also provide some important contextual material for these relationship difficulties. First, there is the impact of economic factors on both the family (in terms of poverty), and the residential care system (in terms of shortage of resources). Second, there is the recognition that the substitute care system faces a major challenge in caring for young people who have already been damaged by their experiences in the family. We return to both these themes in the next chapter.

CHAPTER 6
'Running Away': Synthesis of the Data

Terms such as 'runaways', 'absconders', 'street children', 'young people on the streets' are commonly used to describe the young people covered by this research project. However, none of these terms offers a fully satisfactory definition. The first two (runaways and absconders) refer to an action that a young person may take, and say nothing about the situations they are in after taking that action. The latter two (street children and young people on the streets), on the other hand, describe a situation or lifestyle with no explanation of how that came about.

This problem of definition has long been recognised in the USA, where a number of studies have attempted to draw up a satisfactory description of 'young runaways'. The problem is not merely a semantic one, moreover, for without an adequate definition it is difficult to develop effective service provision, or even to discuss the issue.

The Children's Society's streetwork projects have resolved this problem in different ways. This is discussed in more detail in Chapter 8, but for the time being it is important to note that the two refuge-based projects define their target group both in terms of an event that has occurred (e.g. run away, or forced to leave) and in terms of a situation the young people are in (e.g. at risk). The street-based projects, on the other hand, define their target group only in terms of the young person's situation at the point of contact (e.g. on the street).

It is also necessary to take into account the boundary between running away and homelessness which stems from legal considerations. There is still, to a certain extent, a grey area in the law in relation to 16- and 17-year-olds (see page 3).

DESCRIBING THE YOUNG PEOPLE WITH WHOM THE PROJECTS WORK

A full definition of the young people covered by this study requires a discussion of contexts and situations before leaving family or substitute care; motivations for and meanings of the act of leaving family or substitute care; and the subsequent situations in which young people find themselves. The discussion below builds on previous research on young runaways in Leeds (Rees, 1993).

Contexts and situations before leaving family or substitute care

There are a number of aspects to this. On an individual level, there is a range of factors which can contribute to a young person under 16 leaving where they live:

(a) Factors in the family or substitute care environment:

The evidence presented in Chapters 3 — 5 indicates that many of the young people had severe difficulties in the environment which they left. These can be broadly categorised into physical factors (e.g. violence, sexual abuse, bullying, threats of violence from within or outside the home) which also have an emotional element; and purely emotional factors (e.g. emotional neglect, power struggles, differential treatment of siblings).

(b) Factors outside the home environment:

These can include problems at school, pressure from friends, and 'pull' factors such as the attraction of alternative lifestyles and the sense of freedom.

(c) Broader issues:

Interviews with project staff and other professionals have pointed to a number of broader issues:

- financial pressures on families which heighten tension within the family;
- financial pressures on local authorities which mean that services to young people are under-resourced;
- the legal boundary which can restrict flexibility in routes to independence for young people;
- adults' attitudes towards young people, including current dilemmas about the control and punishment of young people, and the extent to which they should have the right to be involved in decisions about their lives.

All these factors play a part in defining the context in which young people decide to leave family or substitute care.

Motivations and meanings of leaving family or substitute care

The concept of 'motivation' implies that leaving family or substitute care is a rational or 'thought-through' act. However, the fact that only a small number of the young people in the sample planned to run away indicates that this may not always be the case. It seems that most young people nevertheless have some goal in mind when they leave family or substitute care.

The categories of motivations put forward in the Leeds research (Rees, 1993) were: escape; running to something or someone; running away in the hope of changing something; and helping friends. The first two of these categories were the most common in that research, and again appear regularly in the data gathered for this research project. The term 'escape' fits the situations of many young people (particularly those who left violent situations), while the concept of running to something or someone was common amongst young people who had developed alternative networks of support 'on the streets'. This is indicative of the diverse nature of the act of leaving family or substitute care for different young people.

Whichever of the above motivations may be present in particular instances, we must always be aware that the act of leaving family or substitute care can be seen as a positive choice by a young person. It is a way in which they can gain or regain some control of their lives, protect themselves from abuse, and stand up to people who wield more power than they do.

The meaning of the act of leaving family or substitute care also needs to be considered. Whilst most young people appear to leave on the spur of the moment, it is still possible that most weigh up the implications of the act before leaving. The implications for a young person who has already run away many times and has developed survival strategies and support networks are clearly very different from those for a young person who has never run away. Thus the act of leaving will have a diversity of meanings. It is also likely that the meaning will vary according to a young person's culture, ethnicity, socio-economic grouping, gender, sexuality, and the type of accommodation they are leaving. The research also raises an important question as to how young people who cannot run away because of disability, cope with unhappiness and crisis where they live.

Situations whilst away from family or substitute care

The interview and questionnaire data indicate the diversity of situations which young people are in whilst away from family or substitute care. Some young people go immediately to a supportive friend or relative and remain there for the whole time they are away. At the other end of the spectrum, some young people spend extended periods away with no fixed place of residence, relying on street networks and the survival strategies outlined earlier (e.g. theft, begging, sex for money).

SUB-GROUPS OF YOUNG PEOPLE WHO RUN AWAY

The above discussion indicates that there are many categories of running away. In order to bring some order to these categories, we analysed the interview and questionnaire data in an attempt to identify major sub-groupings amongst the young people with whom the projects work. The starting point for this analysis was a study of the descriptive data on life histories of the young people who were interviewed during the research. This study suggested several sub-groups of young people with shared patterns of running away experience. The sub-groups identified were then tested on questionnaire data to explore whether the same differences were present in this sample of young people.

This analysis has enabled us to put forward a model of running away patterns or 'pathways'. However, it is important to acknowledge several limitations to the data collected from young people during the research. First, the data was collected from each young person at only one or two points in time. The patterns we have identified are therefore based on retrospective data rather than on periodic observation. Second, the young people varied in age from 12 to 18 and over. This means that the histories of most of the young people up to 'adulthood' are to varying degrees incomplete. Third, the young people were almost all contacted through the streetwork projects. Other running away patterns may be common amongst the larger population of young runaways.

Bearing these limitations in mind, we present below a summary of the analysis and the model of running away 'pathways' which was developed from it. The model is essentially exploratory and could form a focus for further research.

The interview sample

A study of the 31 young people for whom we had gathered detailed life histories through the interviews revealed four distinct sub-groups of young people, three of which represented young people with experience of running away under the age of 16.

Group A: Young people who had run away fewer than ten times and had not spent long periods away from family or substitute care

There were six young people in this category (four females and two males). They had run away between two and six times. With one exception, they had started running away from the age of 13 onwards, had first run away from family, and had spent little (less than a year) or no time in substitute care.

Three of these young people were under 16 at the time of interview: two were living with family and one in residential care. Three were over 16 and were homeless, living in a hostel, or in independent accommodation.

Group B: Young people who had run away ten times or more but had not spent long continuous periods away from family or substitute care before the age of 16

There were 14 young people in this category (five females and nine males). They had started running away at a wide range of ages from seven to 14 years old, either from family or substitute care. Ten of these young people had spent two years or more in substitute care. These young people had spent regular periods away from home or substitute care, living with friends or other people within their social networks. These periods ranged from a day or two up to six months during any one running away episode.

In terms of current situations at the time of interview, there were three distinct groups amongst these 14 young people:

1. Five young people under 16 who had very recently run away (within the last week) or were currently accommodated in care.

2. Three young people under 16 who had run away or been forced to leave where they lived over a month ago and were currently living with friends. (It is possible that these young people were in the process of becoming detached from support networks).

3. Six young people over 16. Two of these people currently had settled accommodation (family and own flat respectively). The other four were all homeless and two had had no settled accommodation for several years since leaving care close to the age of 16.

Group C: Young people who had spent continuous periods of six months or more away from family or substitute care before the age of 16

We identified this sub-group of seven young people in Chapter 3 (pages 26-27). They had all first run from family at ages ranging from six to 15. Four of them had run away ten times or more, but the other three had only run away between two and four times. They had all been in substitute care, but the periods they had spent there were quite short and two of these young people had only been in care after the period they had spent on the streets.

Four of this group were now over 16 and were all living in independent accommodation (own or partner's flat). Of the under-16-year-olds, two were currently in residential care, and one was living with a girlfriend.

Group D: Young people who had run away or left home around or after the age of 16

There were four people in this category. One had run away briefly at the age of 11, but had then not run away again and had left home at the age of 17, subsequently spending more than two years homeless. One had been thrown out by parents two weeks before her sixteenth birthday. The other two young people had never run away or been forced to leave where they lived before the age of 16 but had become homeless after their sixteenth birthday.

Three of these young people currently had accommodation (friends, flat and hostel) and one was still homeless and on the streets.

Comparison of groups A to C

The data presented above indicated that groups A to C differ in three important respects:

- The young people in group A had first run away at an average of around 13 and a half years old, compared to an average of around 11 years old for the other two groups. They had generally started running away at an older age.

- All but one of group A, and all of group C, had first run away from family, whereas people in group B had started running away from a variety of places, including birth family, residential care and foster care.

- Groups A and C had on average spent little time in substitute care (around eight months and one year respectively). Group B, on the other hand, had spent on average more than four years in substitute care.

Questionnaire data

Having identified these sub-groups amongst the interview sample, we were able to explore whether the differences between them, identified in the above comparison, were also found in the larger sample of young people who had completed questionnaires.

These findings are necessarily more tentative, as we do not have such a detailed overview of the young people's lives. In particular, we could not identify young people from the questionnaire data who had spent continuous periods of more than six months away, as this information was not available. However, we were able to identify people who had spent more than a month away from family or substitute care.

We were able to categorise 86 out of 102 people in the sample. In relation to group A above, there were significant differences within this group between those young people who had first run away three times or fewer, and those who had run away four to nine times. These differences would not have been evident in the interview sample because there were only six people in group A. The differences are large enough to suggest that these are distinct sub-groupings. Thus we now have five sub-groups:

Group 1   Young people who have run away one to three times and have not spent long continuous periods on the streets.

Group 2   Young people who have run away four to nine times and have not spent long continuous periods on the streets.

Group 3   Young people who have run away ten times or more and have not spent long continuous periods on the streets.

Group 4   Young people who have spent a continuous period of at least one month detached from family and substitute care.

Group 5   Young people who have not run away under the age of 16 but have subsequently run away or been homeless.

Age of first running away incident

The average ages of first running away incidents for groups 1 to 4 are shown in Table 6.1.

Table 6.1 Average age of first running away incidents amongst the different sub-groups

Group 1 (1 to 3 running away incidents)	13.6 years old
Group 2 (4 to 9 running away incidents)	12.7 years old
Group 3 (10 or more running away incidents)	10.7 years old
Group 4 (experience of detachment)	11.7 years old

These differences were found to be statistically significant[1]. Thus, there may be a link between the age of first running away and the number of times a young person had run away (although we do not know how many times these young people would subsequently have run away). This comparison therefore supports the evidence from the interview sample.

Where people had first run away from

This comparison did not yield conclusive information. A higher percentage of young people in group 3 (16%) had not first run from family, compared with the other groups (8% to 11%), but this difference was not statistically significant.

Experience of substitute care

Here the findings are very similar to those for the interview sample and were statistically significant[2].

Table 6.2 Extent of experience of substitute care amongst the different sub-groups

	% who had lived in substitute care	% who had lived in substitute care for more than a year
Group 1 (1 to 3 running away incidents)	28%	0%
Group 2 (4 to 9 running away incidents)	57%	14%
Group 3 (10 or more running away incidents)	90%	44%
Group 4 (experience of detachment)	83%	30%

[1] (Kruskal Wallis Test, p = 0.0005)
[2] For the figures in the first column of Table 6.2, the significance using the chi-square test was p = 0.0005).

Comparing groups 1 to 3, it can be seen that people who had run away more times were more likely to have experience of living in substitute care. It can also be seen that young people with experience of detachment were likely to have had less experience of substitute care than those who had run away ten times or more but had no experience of detachment.

Conclusions

The analysis of the interview and questionnaire data enables us to identify some broad sub-groups of young people who differ significantly from one another. In presenting this analysis, we are not suggesting that these groups are fixed and contain different young people. Neither are we suggesting a straightforward causal link between, for example, the number of times a young person had run away and their experience of substitute care. On the contrary, it is possible that the young people in groups 1 to 3 in fact all belong to the same group and have simply been observed at different points along the same running away 'pathway'. The above analysis and the evidence presented elsewhere in the report enables us to draw three tentative conclusions:

- It seems that in many cases there is a link between running away patterns and experience of living in substitute care.

- It seems significant that young people who have spent extended continuous periods away from family and substitute care appear to have not always followed the same pathway: they have not always run away many times, and often have little or no experience of living in substitute care prior to their periods of detachment.

- There is a group of young people (group D and group 5 in the interview and questionnaire samples respectively) who are in contact with the streetwork projects but who have never 'run away'. They may well be part of the city centre 'street culture'.

A MODEL OF RUNNING AWAY 'PATHWAYS'

Recent research carried out in Leeds (Rees, 1993) has suggested that 14% of young people had run away overnight before the age of 16, and a further 17% had run away during the day. Amongst those young people who do run away, most (around 70%) do so only once or twice. Nevertheless, the research suggested that around 4% of young people in urban areas run away more than twice before their sixteenth birthday and around 2% of young people who run away overnight go on to run away as many as ten times or more. As described in the introduction (page 3), we can estimate from these figures that some 10,000 young people from the metropolitan counties of England will run away ten times or more before their sixteenth birthday.

The evidence contained within this report suggests that the young people who have begun to run away repeatedly, with whom the different projects work, are a highly vulnerable group, most having experienced family problems and having lived in substitute care or accommodation at some time in their short lives. The empirical data also leads to a theoretical exploration linking patterns of repeated running away with 'family', 'care', and 'detachment from family and care'. But the concept of 'patterns' should not suggest a simple linear progression from family to detachment. Far from it, for the findings contained in this report point to the complexity of running away patterns.

Drawing upon our current research as well as other completed research into this area, we note the following:

- Most young people (probably 90% or more) begin running away from the family.

- Most young people (around 70%) only run away once or twice and have never lived in substitute care.

- A significant proportion of young people who run away three times or more subsequently live in substitute care. Some stop running away and remain 'in care' or return to the family. Others run away repeatedly from care but remain attached to the 'care system'. Finally, some become detached from substitute care, often very quickly.

- Some young people become detached from the family without going into substitute care.

These findings lead to the following model of the main running away 'pathways' which have been identified by the research:

Figure 6.3 Model of running away pathways

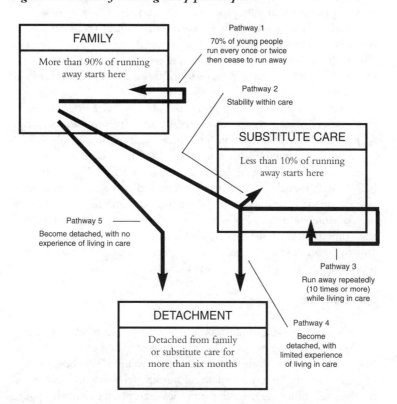

Links between running away patterns and young people's experiences of 'family', 'substitute care' and 'detachment'

The family

Most running away begins in the family (nearly 90% of the young people in the questionnaire sample had first run away from the family) and most young people who run from residential care have run away from their families before entering care. The family is therefore central to any theoretical analysis of running away and this includes a recognition of the complexity, diversity and power dimensions of contemporary family relationships.

In terms of family composition, data from the Family Policy Studies Centre show increases in cohabitation, separation and divorce; the growth of lone parents and reconstituted families; increases in female employment and dual-earner families; as well as ethnic and sexual variations in household forms. Such diversity means that growing numbers of young people find themselves as part of a complex web of social relationships which, depending upon a range of other factors, may be either positive or negative in its consequences. Three-quarters of the interview sample had lived in families where a split had occurred, and in a majority of those cases a step-parent had been introduced.

Significantly, most of the young people researched had, in addition, experienced a misuse of parental power by some combination of physical, sexual and emotional abuse within their families. Violence was a recurring factor leading to many first running away incidents from the family. It was not the only factor, however: 'not being cared about' and 'not being listened to' were also identified by young runaways as important. We cannot say whether there is more or less violence in families where a split has not occurred; only that the combination of changes and splits in the young people's families and different forms of abuse and neglect appears to be a powerful incentive for young people to run away.

Substitute care

As indicated above and illustrated in figure 6.3, around 70% (Rees, 1993) of the young people who run once or twice from their families cease to run away any more. However, around 30% begin to run away repeatedly and most of these young people will spend some time in substitute care. In the interview sample, 86% of the young people who had first run from their families subsequently lived in care. This included young people with long-term care and repeated running away experience (Pathway 3); short-term care and limited running away experience (Pathway 2); and short-term care experience leading to detachment (Pathway 4).

What do we know about the links between care and running away? Completed research (Milham et al., 1986; Rowe et al., 1989) indicates that young people from residential care are over-represented among young people who run away. In comparison with young people who have never been in care, they are more likely to run away at an earlier age and more often. The Leeds survey (Rees, 1993) found that more than one-third of those runaways who had lived in care had run away ten times or more and 7% had only run away once. Of those young people who had never lived in care, however, none had run away as many as ten times and 43% had only run away once. The survey also revealed that young people running from residential care are more likely to run away with someone else, travel further afield, stay away longer and be picked up by the police than young people running away from their families.

Abrahams and Mungall's study indicates wide variations of running away incidents between residential care units of similar sizes, purposes, young people and locations. Earlier UK studies have identified the key role of residential staff in influencing runaway behaviour, including the impact of different levels of control and the significance of positive responses to runaways who return in preventing repeat episodes (Akland, 1981; Milham et al., 1975; Berry, 1975). All the major UK studies highlight the significance of the 14 to 16 age group: "running away is overwhelmingly a problem of middle and late adolescence" (Abrahams and Mungall, page 10, 1992). Rees suggests the need for further research to explore the links between running away episodes and the age of entry to care, length of time in care and the number of different homes a young person had lived in whilst in care.

Our present study identified four common factors leading to young people running away from residential care: feeling that carers did not listen; feeling that carers did not care; being bullied; and suffering violence in care. Other research has added to this picture. Abrahams and Mungall suggest that young people from residential care were often 'running back' to family, friends or previous care placements. They also suggest that various features of 'group living' and the organisation of residential care itself may influence running away behaviour, including: bullying and victimisation; the desire for more individual staff attention; enhancing peer group status; organised 'escapes'; inappropriate placements particularly in cases of young people with severe behavioural difficulties, young offenders and those needing psychiatric treatment; and, finally, the use of distant residential placements. Both Newman (1989) and Rees echo many of these reasons but place more emphasis upon young people's powerlessness and lack of involvement in the care system. At its worst, the whole process of entry to care, the care experience and leaving care can be seen by the young person as outside their control.

Stein (1993) has further developed this theme by suggesting that residential care, under certain conditions, can be a form of 'institutional abuse'. He comments:

"Judged by outcomes this institutional abuse is the chronic failure of much residential child care, (as well as other forms of substitute care) despite the commitment and caring of most of its largely untrained and poorly paid work force, to be a compensatory parent particularly to those young people estranged from their own families who need preparation

> *and support in their transition to adulthood. A growing body of research, powerfully amplified by the voices of young people themselves, shows how substitute care generally fails to compensate and assist them — developmentally, emotionally, educationally — so that by the time they leave care their life chances are very poor indeed.*"

This is not in any way to suggest, simplistically, that care is the cause of the young people's problems, which may be deeply rooted within past family difficulties including damaging and abusive relationships, or that the young people would have been better off if left or returned home. Nor is it to fall into the trap of juxtaposing the 'bad' residential care option with the 'good' fostering option: foster home breakdown rates and unsuccessful outcomes for this age group are similar to residential care, and many young people's substitute care experiences include both foster and residential care (Rowe et al., 1989). In addition, there are, of course, good examples of residential care as well as foster care. Neither is it to ignore the impact of major changes in social legislation and the under-resourcing of public services. Instead, what is being suggested — and supported by our existing knowledge — is that the care system, including residential child care, generally fails to compensate and assist many of these young people. This failure goes far beyond provision in the actual care environment and includes funding policies, training, support and management of carers.

However, simply using the problematic outcomes of residential care experiences as a basis for identifying the phenomenon of 'institutional abuse' is not very helpful in terms of generating a response. We need a working definition.

'Institutional abuse' can be defined as the policies, procedures and practices which create or contribute towards problems of instability, dependency, stigma, identity and under-achievement: the major problem areas highlighted by recent research studies. Against a background of diverse needs, it is difficult to suggest how these problems should be prioritised. But the failure of our system of substitute care to offer many young people stability — that very stability which was often judged to be missing in their own families and backgrounds — raises fundamental questions about the rationale of the system itself.

We know from a number of studies that most young people in long-term care experience multiple placements. Yet such a dispassionate description as 'multiple placements' cannot capture the emotional impact upon young people of changing carers, friends, neighbourhoods and schools, on several occasions, with little constancy in their lives. Neither, despite the resilience of young people, can it capture the emotional energy and strength required by these young people to meet changing expectations derived from new relationships and different social situations. Moreover, these are young people whose own developmental stages have often been impaired or damaged by their pre-care experiences. A rare convergence of sociological, psychological and psychiatric perspectives would conceive being in care, under these conditions, as an assault on personal identity.

Providing stability for young people is therefore prioritised as a prerequisite for addressing the related areas of dependency, stigma, identity and under-achievement. But this is not in any way to downgrade the significance of each of these other dimensions as forms of institutional abuse. They are too important. Dependency and stigma include, for example: policies, procedures and practices from a 'bulk-buying' economy; the denial of personal privacy; and the lack of involvement and participation by young people in decision-making.

Similarly, identity problems may result from a failure to assist young people in gaining essential knowledge and understanding of their cultural, ethnic and family roots. Under-achievement may be connected to a range of institutional care policies and practices, including lack of privacy, low career expectations and poor school links.

A recognition of institutional abuse identifies quality of care as being central to both providing a context for and responding to running away.

Detachment from family and care

Just under a quarter of the young people in the interview sample had spent more than six months continuously away from their families and substitute care before the age of 16. All these young people started running away from their family, and all had spent short periods in care (although not necessarily before the long period that they spent detached). Their 'living' places included all-night venues, friends, empty flats, sleeping rough on the streets and "here, there and everywhere".

Most of these young people had lost contact with education, social services and all other formal agencies, apart from the street-work projects. Self-harm, depression, substance use and involvement in offending were part of their lives. Having left at ages ranging from as young as 11 to 15 years, they were living outside, or marginal to, key societal institutions — their families (or substitute care) and education — the institutions which play such an important role in preparing young people in their transitions to adulthood.

SUMMARY

Detailed analysis of the experience of running away has led us to identify five pathways — with serious (and, for some, apparently irreversible) outcomes. We have also suggested links between patterns of running away and young people's experiences of 'family', 'care' and 'detachment from family and care'. This means we may now be able to find more sensitive and appropriate policy responses. We look at this issue in Chapter 12, after we have explored the current responses of The Children's Society's streetwork projects.

SECTION 2

THE WORK OF THE PROJECTS

CHAPTER 7
Models of Service Provision

This chapter contains a brief description of the direct services offered to young people by each of the four streetwork projects involved in the research project.

YOUTH LINK, BIRMINGHAM

History

In response to The Children's Society's central initiative for 'Young People under Pressure' (see page 5), it was decided to open a project offering a range of services to young people on the streets, through detached work and a drop-in centre. The project officially opened in February 1988.

Methods of work

The project currently works with young people in three connected ways:

(1) *Detached streetwork*

Project workers do detached work in pairs in areas in and around Birmingham city centre where young people are known to spend time. This is done in the afternoons and evenings, on average four times a week. Workers offer support and information to young people and also give them cards with information about the drop-in service (see below). The project works with a range of young people, but one particular target group has been young people who are providing sex for money. An important part of the project's work is to promote safer sexual practices amongst young people on the streets, and a worker employed by a local health authority works with the project and is involved in the detached work.

(2) *Drop-in service*

The drop-in service is open five days a week. It does not operate an open-door policy, but is for young people to use when they have a

71

specific issue or need. The service has practical facilities including a washing machine, showers and toilets, and access to a telephone. There is also a wide range of information on issues relevant to young people. The majority of the young people who use the drop-in have originally had contact with the project workers through the detached work.

(3) *Advocacy*

Linked to the drop-in service, the project offers an advocacy service to young people. Advocacy work attempts to promote the views and interests of the young people, working at their own pace. It also includes encouraging young people to advocate for themselves. The project employs an advocacy specialist who works directly with young people and supports other staff who are doing advocacy work.

Conclusion

The project views the drop-in service and detached work as complementing one another. The detached work is the main initial contact point and the way in which the project workers build up credibility and trust with young people. Its success is therefore vital to the drop-in service. The staff team believe that it would be much more difficult for the drop-in service on its own to establish its credibility and be accessible to young people who spend a lot of time on the streets.

SAFE IN THE CITY, MANCHESTER

History

In response to the 'Young People under Pressure' initiative, the regional manager for the north west of England examined the efficacy of different models of work in the Manchester region. He became aware of the existence of young people aged under 17 on the streets of Manchester and decided to combine an outreach, streetwork model with the development of a small group of foster carers, later known as 'refuge carers'. (Such carers must be approved by The Children's Society as foster carers and by the Department of Health under Section 51 of the Children Act, 1989.)

In 1989, following this initial development work, a project leader was appointed, who began to recruit a team and establish a team base.

Methods of work

The project has adopted three methods of work:

(1) *Streetwork*

The project workers work in pairs on the streets both at predetermined advertised times at fixed venues (known as 'core times') and also at other times which vary. It is on the street that initial contact is made with young people. These contacts can be 'one-off' contacts with young people, or ongoing contacts. The streetworkers carry a 'street bag' which contains practical items such as chocolate, clean underwear and contraceptives. The streetworkers provide practical help, a listening ear and crisis intervention with young people on the street. Between January 1993 and June 1994, the project made contact with 186 young people aged 17 and younger on the streets.

(2) *Advocacy*

Where the project has established ongoing contact with young people, it offers an advocacy service for young people who request this. This service is 'young person-centred': it helps give the young person a voice, helps explore their possible options, and represents their viewpoint to relevant agencies or their family. (The 'young person-centred' approach, which is adopted by all projects, is discussed further on pages 109-112.)

(3) *Refuge*

The original plan for the project to offer refuge with approved foster carers for young people in crisis has proved to be problematic, for reasons internal to and external to The Children's Society. The refuge carers system is therefore non-operative at the time of writing. Between April 1990 and November 1993, young people were offered overnight accommodation within the project on eight occasions.

In addition the project undertakes other activities including:

Networking

The project forms part of a network of projects working with young people in Manchester. This enables the project to share its skills and experiences with other agencies and to learn from and develop in response to other agencies.

Campaigning

As the project has developed, it has increased its campaigning activities in order to try to improve provision for young people.

Links with social services and the police

The project has developed a protocol which has been shared with the local social services department and the police. This states that:

> *"Safe in the City will reach and work with young people aged 17 years and under who are estranged and adrift in the city of Manchester. The project can offer support and advice, mediation and negotiation in the process of reuniting the young people to caring, responsible adult support. Where a young person is at risk of harm the project can provide a safe refuge as provided in the regulations for Section 51: Refuge for young people at risk: the 1989 Children Act."*

Conclusion

Safe in the City has developed a radical new approach to streetwork with a high emphasis on detached streetwork, which utilises a combination of youth work and social work approaches. It places a high value on its 'young person-centred' approach and attempts to ensure that all policies are consistent with this central philosophy.

Safe in the City is currently considering the future direction of the project. The fact that the project has so far managed without refuge carers has raised the possibility that it can continue to survive without any or with only a small number of refuge carers. Many project workers are also keen to develop the campaigning work they undertake.

LEEDS SAFE HOUSE

History

In response to the streetwork initiative, the north east region of The Children's Society carried out two pieces of research — in Leeds and Newcastle — to examine the needs of young people who run away and to explore responses to their needs. The outcome of this research was the decision to set up a residential refuge in Leeds targeted at young people who had run away or been forced to leave where they live.

A project leader was appointed in 1989. Premises were found, and the rest of the staff team appointed in 1990. The refuge opened to young people in February 1991.

Methods of work

(1) *24-hour telephone contact and referral*

Due to the confidential location of the refuge, initial contact for young people or agencies is by telephone, staffed 24 hours a day. At this stage a project worker will offer a listening ear to the young person and establish whether her/his situation fits the basic criteria for refuge as follows:

young people under 16 who have:

–   left their usual or last place of residence without permission and are unwilling to return, or

–   been forced to leave against their will, and

–   made a positive decision to be at the Safe House.

In special circumstances Leeds Safe House will also work with 16- and 17-year-olds who fit these criteria if they are seeking refuge from a person(s) who is likely to cause them significant harm.

   If these criteria are met, the worker will usually arrange to meet the young person and discuss the situation further. This is usually followed by the young person being brought into refuge. If a bed space is not available the worker will offer support to the young person and information about other agencies who may be able to offer help. The refuge is registered as a children's home.

(2) *Refuge*

The refuge is staffed by a minimum of two workers, 24 hours a day, and can accommodate six young people at any one time. Practical facilities such as food, pocket money, washing facilities and a change of clothes are available. Work in the refuge is done in a highly structured way. Young people are encouraged to explore their options, and this is often followed by telephone contact or meetings with parents or social services.

The refuge operates according to the regulations set down in Section 51 of the Children Act 1989, which means that it can accommodate a young person for up to 14 days in the first instance, and for a total of no more than 21 days in any three-month period.

(3) *Follow-up work*

The philosophy of the project is one of short-term crisis intervention. Thus extended follow-up work is not undertaken with young people after they leave the refuge. Young people are offered one visit or meeting, and may also continue to have telephone contact with the project.

In addition to these areas of direct work with individual young people, the project has an ongoing programme of research and evaluation, and also aims to undertake campaigning work on issues affecting the young people with whom it works.

Links with social services and the police

The project is currently negotiating protocol agreements with the local social services department and the police. In addition, due to its refuge service, it has close links with the Social Services Inspectorate.

Conclusion

Having been in operation for over three years as a refuge service, the project is currently evaluating its work in order to learn from its experience and explore potential new initiatives for working with young people in its target group. This may include doing more preventative work with young people in relation to running away.

As with the other projects, Leeds Safe House sees its 'young person-centred' approach as being a fundamental aspect of its work.

THE PORTH PROJECT, GWENT

History

The Porth Project is the most recent addition to the streetwork programme. Its establishment followed research in Wales, carried out for The Children's Society by Swansea University, which indicated a significant incidence of young people running away in a number of parts of the country. It was decided to set up the project in a town where there is a perceived lack of a range of services for young people. At this stage there were already two residential-style refuges in operation in England, so it was decided to explore the more community-based response of refuge carers, similar to that originally planned by Safe in the City. It was also intended that an information service for young people should be opened. Due to the shortage of available resources, however, the development of this service was subsequently postponed and is currently on hold.

The Porth refuge carers became the first in England and Wales to be granted a certificate under Section 51 of the Children Act. The first certificate was issued by the Welsh Office in April 1993.

The project started working with young people in refuge in July 1993.

Methods of work

(1) *24-hour telephone contact and referral*

As with Leeds Safe House, the project is accessible by telephone 24 hours a day. On receiving a referral, workers will offer the young person support and, if there is a bed space available and the young person fits the referral criteria, arrange to meet them.

The project will only accept referrals where the following conditions are met:

—   A referral being made on behalf of a young person has the active support of the young person in question.

—   A young person is aged 15 and under and has currently run away from, or is refusing to return to, the family home/responsible person.

—   The young person is aged 17 years and under and is in the care of a local authority, from where s/he has currently run away, or is refusing to return.

—   A young person must appear to be at risk of harm and would continue to be at risk of harm if refuge is not provided.

At the meeting between the young person and the project worker, the young person's situation is discussed further and, as far as is practical, s/he is offered a choice of refuge carers.

(2) *Refuge carers*

The project has six refuge carers/families at confidential locations, who have been approved as foster carers by The Children's Society and certificated as refuges by the Welsh Office. The refuge carers accommodate the young people at evenings and overnight, and all day at weekends, and offer practical and emotional support to young people. One of the main roles of the deputy project leader is to support refuge carers through the approval and certification processes (which can take up to a year) and when they have young people in refuge.

(3) *The office base*

The project's office base is also certificated as a refuge. During the daytime on weekdays young people are brought from the refuge carers to the office, where project workers support them in exploring their situation and the options that are open to them. This will often be followed by advocacy, mediation or negotiation work.

(4) *Follow-up support*

As with Leeds Safe House, the project sees itself as offering short-term intervention and only provides limited follow-up support to young people after they leave the refuge.

Research and evaluation

In addition to the direct work with young people, the project employed a research worker on a fixed-term contract to carry out a study of homelessness and running away amongst young black people in Newport (Patel, 1994).

The project also has an evaluation programme in conjunction with Lancaster University.

Links with other agencies

The project has protocol agreements with the local social services department and the police, and has a working relationship with the

Welsh Office. The regional social work manager with responsibility for the project sits on the local Area Child Protection Committee (ACPC).

Conclusion

At the time of writing, the refuge service has been running for 12 months. It is therefore too early to draw conclusions about the service. Early indications are that, whilst the service provision differs, the young people and issues with which the project works are similar to those at Leeds Safe House.

CHAPTER 8
Comparison of the Young People in Contact with the Projects

COMPARISON OF CHARACTERISTICS AND EXPERIENCES

From the questionnaire data and project statistices it was possible to make comparisons between the young people who use all four of the projects. Some of the main characteristics and experiences are summarised in the table below. (Where indicated by a ★ the data was gathered from project statistics; in the other cases the questionnaire data is used.)

Table 8.1 *A comparison of the characteristics of the young people with whom the projects work*

	Leeds Safe House	Porth Project	Safe in the City	Youth Link
Age	Almost all (95%) under 16	Mostly (80%) under 16★	Wide range of ages, 12 to 17 and over	Wide range of ages, 13 to 17 and over
Sex	More females (68%) than males	More females (69%) than males★	Slightly more females (57%) than males	More males (63%) than females
Ethnic origin	Mostly white – some evidence of use by young people from ethnic minorities	Mostly white – some evidence of use by young people from ethnic minorities	Mostly white – some evidence of use by young people of mixed origin	Mostly white – some evidence, from project statistics, of use by young people from ethnic minorities
Sexuality	Inadequate data	Inadequate data	Inadequate data	Some evidence of use by gay young men
Current situation	All had either run away (86%) or had been forced to leave where they lived (14%)	All had either run away (94%) or had been forced to leave where they lived (6%)★	Almost half (48%) currently had somewhere to live	Two-fifths (39%) currently had somewhere to live
Current or most recent accommodation	Most family (71%)	Slightly more family (56%) than substitute care (44%)★	Mostly in residential care	Wide range but relatively small proportion in residential care (11%)
Care experience	Around half of sample (55%), many for short periods	Around half of sample★	89%, often for long periods of time	Around three-quarters of sample (71%)
Involvement in prostitution	Inadequate data	Inadequate data	Inadequate data	Over a quarter of the sample (mainly male)

Clearly, there are significant differences between the young people with whom the projects work and, in particular, between the refuge-based services and street-based services.

The refuges in Leeds and South Wales work with a more tightly defined group of young people in terms of age and current situation. This is due to the tight referral criteria and 'gate-keeping' aspect of the projects' working models. The differences between the two street-based projects in terms of young people's ethnic origin, sexuality and care experience may reflect differences in the local situations in the two cities rather than differences that can be attributed to their different models of service provision.

COMPARISON OF RUNNING AWAY EXPERIENCES

We can go on to compare running away experiences amongst the young people in contact with three of the different projects using the sub-groupings identified in Chapter 6 (pages 56 - 61). The breakdown of the interview and questionnaire samples was as follows:

Table 8.2   The running away experience of young people using the projects

a) Interview sample:

Group	Description	Leeds Safe House	Safe in the City	Youth Link
Group A	Run away nine times or less, no extended periods away	3	1	2
Group B	Run away more than ten times, no extended periods away	5	4	5
Group C	Had spent a period of a month or more away from family or care	0	3	4
Group D	Little or no running away, homelessness just before or after 16	0	1	3

b) Questionnaire sample[1]:

Group	Description	Leeds Safe House	Safe in the City	Youth Link
Group 1	Run away three times or less, no extended periods away	14 (34%)	1 (5%)	2 (10%)
Group 2	Run away four to nine times, no extended periods away	10 (24%)	2 (10%)	1 (5%)
Group 3	Run away more than ten times, no extended periods away	12 (29%)	6 (29%)	0
Group 4	Had spent a period of a month or more away from family or care	3 (7%)	8 (38%)	13 (62%)
Group 5	Little or no running away, homelessness just before or after 16	2 (5%)	4 (19%)	5 (24%)

[1] The figures in table (b) do not tally with those on Table 6.1 because they exclude young people in contact with the Porth Project.

Again, there are strong differences between the refuge in Leeds and the two street-based projects: 58% of the Leeds questionnaire sample were in groups 1a and 1b, compared with 15% in both of the street-based projects. This would indicate that Leeds Safe House works with much larger proportions of young people earlier on in the running away 'pathways' identified in Chapter 6 (see page 63). The differences between Safe in the City and Youth Link in terms of groups 2 and 3 appear to be significant from the questionnaire sample, but should not be regarded as such in view of the tentative nature of the categorisation.

Interestingly, however, the differences in overall running away experiences between Leeds and the other two projects are not as large as might have been expected from the above comparison. For example, we found no evidence of a statistical difference in terms of such indicators as sleeping rough and travelling outside the local area whilst running away, nor amongst most of the indicators of positive and negative experiences described in Chapter 4 (pages 42 - 43).

This lack of evidence of differences in experiences is partly attributable to the size of the questionnaire sample, which makes detection of statistically significant differences less likely. The main statistical difference we did find, however, was in the number of times young people had run away: the young people in the Leeds Safe House sample had run away fewer times on average, although it should also be noted that the average age in this sample was 14.4 years old, compared with over 16 years old in the samples of both the street-based projects.

Nevertheless, even in the Leeds sample, the majority of young people (57%) had run away four times or more. In comparison, the recent Children's Society's survey of a representative sample of young people throughout the city (Rees, 1993), showed that 16% of those who had run away had done so four times or more. Therefore, even though Leeds Safe House is working with more young people who are earlier on in the running away 'pathways' than the street-based projects, it too is predominantly focused on young people who are already regularly running away.

We return to the subject of differences between the projects' groups of service users and their relative accessibility in Chapter 11 and discuss the policy implications of the findings in Chapter 13.

CHAPTER 9
Outcomes of the Projects' Work

This section does not offer a comprehensive evaluation of the projects' work, but rather an exploration of the potential of each of the models currently in operation, and an outline of some of the key issues that have arisen through the work of the projects.

We concentrate, in this chapter, on the concept of outcomes which has been a central part of the research methodology outlined in the introduction to the report. Broadly speaking, **an outcome is defined as a result of a project's work which the project sets out to achieve, and for which it can plausibly be held accountable.**

An analysis of the outcomes models drawn up for the projects suggests four main categories of general outcomes of direct work with young people, which all the projects were working on in one form or another:

1. Catering for young people's immediate needs.
2. Establishing a positive relationship with young people.
3. Facilitating change in young people's situations.
4. Attending to young people's long-term needs.

Thus the research methodology focused on assessing the impact of the projects' work in these four broad areas. The discussion below is based on information from young people contacted through three of the projects (Youth Link, Safe in the City, and Leeds Safe House), and from staff and professionals in other agencies connected with all four projects. In view of the relatively small number of young people interviewed at the two refuge-based projects, we have also made some limited use of project records as supplementary information.

CATERING FOR YOUNG PEOPLE'S IMMEDIATE NEEDS

Catering for young people's needs while they are away from family or substitute care or on the streets can broadly be broken down into the following specific outcomes:

- Catering for material needs (e.g. a place to sleep or hide, food, clothes, hygiene, health needs, information).

- Catering for emotional needs (e.g. someone to talk to, to feel safe).

Whilst all the projects aimed to meet at least some of these needs, there were differences in emphasis, particularly concerning the issue of young people's safety.

Refuge-based projects

There is no significant difference in the range of immediate needs that the Porth Project and Leeds Safe House aim to meet, and so we have considered them together here. Both projects aim to meet all of the needs outlined above.

The projects provide for the material needs of the young people they accept into refuge as a matter of course, offering them a place to sleep, food and clothes. They therefore achieve the outcomes set out with these young people and are clearly providing a valuable service for the young people they work with. However, in both projects the demand for refuge bed spaces has often been greater than the supply. As a result, the projects are unable to meet the needs of all the young people who contact them, within their existing resources. There is also a question as to whether the young people are always in need of these services, and in particular a place to sleep (see pages 88 – 89).

Seven of the eight young people interviewed at Leeds Safe House made positive comments in relation to their immediate needs being met, particularly emphasising their feelings of safety at the refuge and the short-term emotional support they received:

> *"They took me in. They've looked after me. They cared about me. They worried about me. They won't let me take my tablets when I want to overdose. They stop me doing stupid things."*

The immediate care and protection that the refuges can provide were seen as important aspects of the service by staff in both the projects, and this was backed up by a number of comments from professionals in other agencies who welcomed the services the refuges were providing:

> *"It's been helpful because she would be genuinely at risk* [of being involved in prostitution] *if Porth wasn't there."*

"It's a haven, somewhere they can feel safe for a period of time, and look at solutions .... I feel relieved that there is something like the Safe House."

"Children are being taken off the streets. It's something that the bobbies on the ground have seen the need for."

Drop-in service

The research at Youth Link focused on young people who used the drop-in service. This service offers a range of practical facilities which are designed to meet young people's immediate needs, together with the opportunity to have a break from the streets and to talk. The staff saw the provision of washing facilities, in particular, as a way of enabling young people on the streets to maintain their self-esteem. The drop-in centre also has a wide range of information which is accessible to young people.

Four of the young people interviewed made specific mention of valuing the practical services provided and the opportunity to talk to someone whom they could trust, whilst there were also examples of how the drop-in's regular accessibility was helpful to young people in a crisis situation. One young person had found the immediate support offered by the drop-in helpful when he had taken an overdose, and in another case a young person of 14 who had been thrown out of home contacted the drop-in and was found accommodation for that night.

"They sit down and listen to you ... give you advice and say you don't have to take it."

"I'm glad I found out about Youth Link so I could contact my parents."

Street-based services

Both Safe in the City and Youth Link aim to cater for young people's material needs whilst on the street (e.g. food, health needs, information) and offer a point of contact for young people. A number of young people in both projects commented that they had valued the help the project workers had given them on the streets, and the opportunity to talk. However, some needs are clearly difficult to meet on the streets (e.g. facilities to wash).

"The children never have anywhere to go ... there should be more people like Safe in the City."

"They are good to talk to."

The projects also aim, through their detached work, to promote the safety of young people in their current environment. There is some evidence from the research that the projects are able to do this through the presence of workers on the street, and by working with young people to develop strategies for safety (e.g. safe sex for those involved in prostitution):

> *"I would just like to say that Safe in the City saved my neck many a time, they've given me advice on all my problems, and I would like to say thanks."*

There may be limits, however, to the level of safety that can be achieved on the streets. Amongst the questionnaire sample in Manchester and Birmingham, 37% had been frightened while on the streets, 30% had been physically assaulted, and 13% had been sexually assaulted. Thus clearly there are significant risks involved in spending time on the streets. Most of the young people in the interview sample had adopted survival strategies such as begging, stealing or prostitution to survive on the streets. In the questionnaire sample, 64% of young people in Manchester and Birmingham had stolen or shoplifted while on the streets and 21% had been involved in prostitution. Finally, the majority of the interview samples in Manchester and Birmingham had sometimes or usually needed a place to stay while on the streets, and had often slept rough.

Discussion

All the projects appeared to achieve the outcomes aimed for in catering for young people's immediate needs. However, the range of needs catered for varied, reflecting a difference in emphasis between the projects with regard to offering young people accommodation, refuge, and safety. This is an important area for debate when considering the development of services.

The interviews offered evidence of a significant need for accommodation and physical safety amongst the young people in contact with all the projects. The issue remains of how this may suitably be provided. The highly structured refuge service offered by Leeds Safe House and the Porth Project can be effective in this respect but also has other effects (see pages 99–101) and may not always be attractive to young people who spend a lot of time on the streets. On the other hand, the presence of street-based workers may not always be sufficient in itself to ensure young people's safety and there will be times when young people on the streets need some means of respite. The possibility of emergency accommodation facilities (linked with a 24-hour telephone contact point) or night-time drop-in services could be explored.

The ability of the projects to cater for the immediate needs of young people was welcomed by many professionals in statutory agencies.

ESTABLISHING A POSITIVE RELATIONSHIP WITH YOUNG PEOPLE

All the projects saw the establishment of a positive relationship with young people as a necessary prerequisite to the other work they aimed to do with them. This outcome forms a crucial aspect of the 'young person-centred' approach we discuss in Chapter 10.

The young people in the interview sample were asked to complete a grid outlining how they saw their relationship with the project staff, which included the five statements also covered for social workers (see page 30). There were no significant differences between projects and the large majority of young people evaluated the project staff positively on the issues covered:

Table 9.1 Interviewed young people's responses about project staff

	Yes	Some-times	No
1. The workers take what I say seriously.	22	1	0
2. The workers do things behind your back.	0	2	21
3. The workers ignore what I tell them.	0	22	0
4. If I have a problem I feel I can talk to a worker about it.	19	2	2
5. The workers let me make my own decisions.	16	2	0
6. The project is on young people's side.	20	2	0
7. The project is there when you need it.	17	4	1
8. The workers understand young people.	14	1	0

We were able to compare the responses of 16 people to statements one to five above with their responses to the same five questions relating to their social workers. Of course, this comparison needs to be put into context. First, project workers have none of the statutory duties or powers that social workers have which, for instance, may not allow social workers to let young people make their own decisions about certain matters; nor do they have the care and control role with which field and residential social workers are identified. Second, the project has a range of workers available to young people, whereas the young person will only have one social worker. Third, the interview sample was inherently biased in that all the young people were contacted through the streetwork projects, and most had had a lengthy relationship with the projects. There may be other young people who were not so positive about the projects and had therefore only contacted them once or twice.

It is perhaps not surprising then that a statistical test indicates that young people had a significantly more positive attitude to project workers than to social workers on all five scales. Nevertheless, it is a significant achievement by the projects that they were all able to establish such positive relationships with young people who are often marginalised and do not have a positive relationship with other adults (as shown in Chapter 3).

A selection of comments from young people illustrate this achievement:

> "They just don't pressure you like social workers do. That's why I like them." (young person in Manchester)

> "You can say what you like. You know it won't go beyond the walls." (young person in Birmingham)

> "You get to know them. You get close to the workers. You learn to trust them and they trust you." (young person in Leeds)

The issue of trust is apparent in two of the above quotes and was a recurring theme of young people's comments about all the projects. A vital component of this trust appears to be the projects' confidentiality and open records policies. We discuss the issue of confidentiality in more detail in Chapter 11.

FACILITATING CHANGE IN YOUNG PEOPLE'S SITUATIONS

The outcome of facilitating change in the young person's situation is central to the functioning of all the streetwork projects. In order to understand this issue in more depth we have subdivided 'change' into the following categories:

Systems intervention: As we have already established, two-thirds of the young people in the interview sample were currently in contact with a parent, but most of these relationships were poor and/or infrequent. Young people sometimes ask projects to re-establish contact with parents or to negotiate on their behalf in relation to an issue or problem which has arisen. We have also established that most of the interview sample had experience of living in substitute care. Again the quality of young people's relationships with both care staff and field staff is reported by young people to be poor. Project staff are therefore often drawn into negotiations with care and field staff aimed at planning a return to placement or a new placement for a young person. Project staff also negotiate with other systems, including the criminal justice, housing, social security and health systems.

Supporting personal change and growth: Project workers play a key role in supporting change by the young person. In keeping with the 'young person-centred' approach this work is only undertaken when the young person wishes the change to take place. The levels and nature of this change vary considerably, but examples include behavioural change including safe sex, and skill development including self-advocacy skills.

Supporting informed-decision making: All projects aim to provide young people with information that enables the young person to reach an informed decision. This process involves the young person/worker identifying the issue; the worker providing — or encouraging the young person to gather — the relevant information; the young person/worker exploring the various options; the young person reaching a decision supported and facilitated by the project worker.

We again deal with each type of service provision in turn:

Refuge-based services

The two refuge-based services work intensively with young people over a short period of time (up to 14 days). This fits into a model of short-term crisis intervention and allows the potential for considerable change to be made in key areas of young people's lives. Six of the eight young people interviewed at Leeds Safe House felt that the project had helped them to achieve changes that they wanted. These changes related predominantly to systems intervention with the social services department, but there was also evidence of perceived personal change, and of reconciliations with family:

> *"They built my self-confidence so that I could say what I wanted to say."*

> *"I just want to write that we all know that life isn't easy even for parents, but we young people do go through a lot and most of the time people don't listen to us, but now the Safe House is open a lot of young people have sorted their lives out and some are still with their natural parents because of the fact the Safe House listens and understands and helps us. They also love and care for us and they show it."*

All six young people had had meetings with social services supported by project workers whilst at the refuge. In four cases the young people had run from residential care and the meetings addressed issues of bullying and treatment in residential care. In the other two cases the young people had run from family, and the meetings involved engaging the young person with social services and exploring accommodation options. Although the outcomes of these meetings appear to have been mixed, the young people valued the support they got from project workers and the opportunity to have their views heard.

Comments from external professionals in Leeds and South Wales indicate that the ability of the refuge-based projects to facilitate positive change in young people's lives is recognised by outside agencies:

> *"I think workers do good work with them. I know they did some very good work with her on her feelings which she found useful."*

> *"They made us do something about her situation. We knew [Children's Home] wasn't a good place to be, but because she changed her story and it was difficult to find her a place she was left there longer than she should have been. Porth caused us to do something .... It gave her somewhere to go when she felt she had no control of her life."*

> *"One young person couldn't cope. [The streetwork project] helped him move on in a way that the social services department couldn't have. It was a decision of life and death and I honestly think he would have gone off and killed himself. He's now got a flat."*

As only a small number of young people contributing to this section were from the refuge-based projects, we supplemented the above information with an analysis of a sample of recent stays at Leeds Safe House. (We believe that the potential outcomes at the two refuge-based projects are broadly similar, although the services differ in other ways.) A 25% sample of stays during January to June 1994 were looked at: 34 stays in total. Thirteen of these stays ended with the young person choosing to leave the refuge within the first two days (often young people who had used the refuge a number of times). These included four young people who had spent extended periods on the streets away from family or substitute care. In these cases there was little evidence of major change, although the stay had allowed young people temporary respite from their situation and the opportunity to talk. The remaining 21 stays all provided evidence of work on change.

Eight of these young people had run from residential care, of whom six returned to their placement after phone calls or meetings which appeared to have resolved at least some of the issues which had led them to run away. The remaining two were found foster carers and a family placement respectively, after meetings with social services.

Eleven young people had run from parents. In five cases the young people returned home after phone calls and meetings to negotiate with the family. Four young people were found alternative placements (foster care, relative, friend, and hostel) after exploration of accommodation options with the young person, social services and relatives. One young person left without informing the staff, and one had to leave the refuge due to a breach of rules.

Finally, one young person who had been living on the streets was found a residential care placement, and one young person who had run from relatives other than parents and was about to reach 16 years of age was found a place in a hostel.

This analysis of stays indicates the potential of refuge-based projects to work intensively with young people to find solutions to their situations. In some cases this means a negotiated return to family or substitute care after having resolved some of the issues that led to the young person leaving. In other cases this means finding an alternative place to live (e.g. substitute care, relatives, hostels) which the young person is happy with.

In addition to work on move-on options, work had been done with five young people on school issues (including meetings with school staff and education welfare officers), with two young people on health issues (including accompanying to hospital), and with two young people on legal issues (including attending court with a young person).

Drop-in service

The drop-in service at Youth Link enables workers to spend focused time with young people working on issues that are concerning them, with access to a wide range of information and the ability to contact other agencies by telephone or to support the young person in doing this themselves. The presence of an advocacy specialist at Youth Link was seen by staff as a vital resource in enabling the project to facilitate change in young people's lives. The advocacy specialist works directly with some young people, and in other cases acts as a source of information and advice for other staff working with young people.

Twelve of the 14 young people interviewed identified ways in which they felt Youth Link had helped them. The range of issues worked with was wide, and most people mentioned more than one issue. These included:

- benefits (seven people): including informing young people of their entitlements, contacting the Department of Social Security, and encouraging self-advocacy;

- accommodation (six people): five of whom the project had helped to find somewhere to live;

- contact and meetings with social services (four people): including attending reviews and case conferences in support of the young person;

- legal issues (four people): including enabling young people to learn about their rights, and supporting young people in court;

- contact with parents (four people): usually enabling young people to regain contact with their parents (see also next section);

- health (two people): setting up appointments and accompanying people to them.

A quote from a young person illustrates the way in which the drop-in service works:

> *"They've helped with benefits and entitlements, it's impossible for me to know social security inside out. They've helped to give me the confidence to do something about legal options. I knew I was doing some-*

thing legally. They've helped to make a lot of decisions ... explain the good and bad points ... never push me."

Little information relevant to the areas being discussed was gathered from other professionals in Birmingham.

Street-based work

The fact that project staff are on the street enables them to work with young people to facilitate change on territory that is familiar to the young person, and at a pace that is dictated by the young person. These are important positives to the street-based approach, but it also seems that the work on facilitating change which workers are able to achieve on the streets may be more limited than in the two other service settings described above. There are practical reasons for this: street-based work is often done in the evenings when most other agencies are not available; the amount of information which workers can carry with them on rights and entitlements is limited; and the environment itself is not always conducive to structured work with young people.

There were therefore few examples from the young people interviewed in Manchester and Birmingham of major changes (of the kind outlined in the previous sections) being achieved on the streets, although young people did value the opportunity to discuss their problems with workers and often felt that this had enabled them to come to decisions. Safe in the City does, however, engage in advocacy work and systems intervention in addition to its street-based work, and there were several examples of the potential of this aspect of the project's work to facilitate change: for example, negotiating with the Department of Social Security and helping a young person with a solicitor.

"They helped me to see a solicitor and see about a private tutor."

ATTENDING TO YOUNG PEOPLE'S LONG-TERM NEEDS

All the projects, and indeed the legal framework of Section 51 of the 1989 Children Act, are established to ensure that the projects address immediate or short-term needs. This style of work fits functionally with the idea of crisis 'streetwork' or short-term 'refuge'. Long-term work is therefore structurally more difficult for the project to achieve. (This is reflected in the logistical problems the research team had in contacting young people for second stage interviews.) Additionally, there was an ongoing debate in the projects about the extent to which they should become involved with young people on a long-term basis, given their focus on crisis intervention. The projects therefore most often aimed to establish other networks to meet young people's longer-term needs, rather than attempting to meet these needs themselves.

The projects saw one of the possible outcomes of their work as acting as a bridge or link in order to re-establish contact between the young people and their families or other agencies. This is an important area of their work and the projects hold that the 'young person-centred' or 'advocacy' approach they adopt is an essential part of it. This approach can also be difficult, however, as some other agencies hold hostile conceptions of the projects (partly due to this approach, as discussed in Chapter 11) and are sometimes reluctant to work constructively with them.

The data gathered indicates that the projects involved in refuge-based or drop-in services were often able to provide an essential link between a young person and other more long-term support networks. This is illustrated in a number of examples in the above sections, where refuge-based projects were able to help young people re-establish contact with carers (either family or substitute care). Four of the 14 young people who had used the drop-in service at Youth Link said that the project had helped them to regain links with their parents. Additionally there was some evidence of all the projects encouraging young people to establish links with other agencies, although this was sometimes met with reluctance by the young person:

> *"They suggested* [a counselling project] *but going to a place like that means you've got a problem. You don't know what people will be like and it's difficult to go in for the first time. There's not much chance of support from my social worker. So I'll probably ring up the Safe House."*

This quote illustrates that, whilst the projects have been highly successful in establishing trusting relationships with young people, the young people are still reluctant to put their trust in other organisations. Perhaps partly for this reason, all the projects become involved with some young people on a long-term basis. This involvement manifests itself in different ways according to the service setting.

The refuge-based projects offer limited follow-on support to young people after they have left the refuge. However, young people often return on more than one occasion. Seven of the eight young people interviewed at Leeds Safe House had stayed at the refuge more than once, some more than ten times over a period of several years. Project statistics indicate that over half the young people who stay at the refuge return for a second stay. In addition, many young people contact the project by telephone for support in between stays. Although the Porth Project has not been established for as long as Leeds Safe House, it has already worked with several young people on more than one occasion.

The drop-in and street-based projects have a more open-ended relationship with young people. Four of the ten young people interviewed at Manchester had had contact with Safe in the City for more than two years, and the remaining six had all had contact regularly for at least three months. In Birmingham, seven of the 14 young people interviewed had been in contact sporadically or regularly with Youth Link for more than two years, and a further five for at least three months. Two were interviewed during their first contact with the project. In addition, both projects have visited young people they have had contact with when they have been in other settings (e.g. children's homes, secure accommodation, hospital), and this aspect of the work is particularly valued by the young people concerned:

> "I still see them a lot. They came to see me in hospital ... they got in contact with me through my social worker. I rang them up to tell them about the baby. [Project worker] brought me some baby clothes and [another project worker] helped too."

Thus it is apparent that all four of the projects have become involved on a longer-term basis with some of the young people they work with. This involvement is often highly valued by the young people:

> "Without the support and help I received from Youth Link, from a hot cup of tea and a shower to someone to talk to, I wouldn't have been able to sort out the problems I've had. I feel that the ongoing help and support I've received from Youth Link has helped me gain the settled secure life I now lead."

However, it is not consistent with a short-term crisis intervention approach. It was evident from interviews with project staff that this issue has been recognised by all the projects and has been the subject of much debate.

SUMMARY

There is evidence that all four projects have had significant success in achieving their stated outcomes in direct work with young people.

In terms of the first category of stated outcomes — catering for young people's immediate needs — all the projects appear to be meeting their objectives. There is a difference in emphasis, with the refuge-based services aiming to offer an alternative to being on the streets, whilst the street-based projects aim to support young people in their current situation on the streets.

The projects have been conspicuously successful in the second category of outcomes: establishing a positive relationship with young people. This is a significant achievement, considering many of the young people's detachment from, and distrust of, adults in general.

All the projects have been able to facilitate positive change in young people's lives, while working to young people's agendas: the third category of outcomes. There are again differences between the projects, with the refuge-based services able to achieve major life changes through their short-term intensive work with young people. The drop-in service was also able to assist in significant changes for young people through the range of facilities it offers.

The findings for the fourth category of outcomes — relating to young people's longer-term needs — were more complex. The projects have had some success in establishing links between young people and families or agencies, thus ensuring that young people's longer-term needs are met. However, there seem to be at least two barriers to this process in many cases: young people's distrust of other organisations; and conflict between some organisations and the streetwork projects. There are indications therefore that all the projects are developing long-term relationships with young people, which may not always be in keeping with the original philosophies of the projects.

CHAPTER 10
Effects of the Projects' Work

The work of the projects may have unintended or unanticipated effects on the young people, on project staff and on others external to the project. The evidence for these effects, which may be either positive or negative, is based predominantly on the interviews with project staff and external professionals.

EFFECTS ON YOUNG PEOPLE

There are some issues which were common to more than one project, but we deal first with effects specific to each particular service model.

Residential refuge-based work

Some staff identified possible positive effects. For example:

- enabling young people to make peer group friendships with others who have been through similar experiences, which provide a young person with support during their stay and after leaving;

- giving young people a positive experience of adults;

- introducing young people to different cultures and ways of being.

There were several commonly-held concerns amongst project staff about potential negative effects on young people specifically related to the residential model. These were:

- young people from different backgrounds coming together, leading to some young people being introduced to offending, drug and substance use by other young people whilst at the refuge;

- the negatives of being in crisis with other young people in crisis;

- the rules necessary to run a residential establishment leading to young people being barred from access to the refuge due to breaking the rules. This was also a concern of some professionals in other agencies in Leeds:

> *"The residential setting presents a problem for some, if not all, young people. They come in with certain things they want to change, being in a refuge situation detracts from what they came in for. Individual needs tend to take on less importance than what's going on in the house. Interactions can be detrimental."*

Dispersed refuge-based work

The dispersed refuge model operated by the Porth Project avoids the above negative effects by providing individual accommodation for young people and thus also limiting the extent to which young people in refuge mix with each other. The staff and refuge carers felt that a potential positive effect of this model is for young people to experience good parenting (possibly for the first time) when in refuge.

A potential negative effect of the model arose during a number of the interviews with staff and refuge carers. This was the possibility that young people in crisis would form a strong relationship with refuge carers in a short period of time, which gave them difficulties or led to them feeling rejected when they left the refuge.

Refuge-based work (general)

Some potential effects are relevant to both types of refuge-based work.

The intensive nature of short-term refuge work can have a beneficial effect in various ways: for example, giving young people an experience of belonging, and enhancing their self-esteem.

This intense relationship can also have drawbacks, however:

- Staff expressed concerns about how young people might feel when they had to leave the refuge after 14 days and were offered only limited follow-up support:

> *"I think it's very hard for young people to let go of the project; being concentrated on short-term crisis intervention, young people can feel abandoned at the end of their stay here."*

- There were also some worries about potential effects for young people when they returned to the place they had run away from. Some staff feared, for example, that Asian young people may have suffered repercussions on returning home, due to the fact that they had stayed at a refuge. Staff also expressed concern about young people who had run from an abusive situation and had to return there after being in refuge.

- A common concern amongst external professionals in social services was the possibility that stays in refuge by young people in substitute care might have disrupted long-term care plans for them, such as a return home from care, or an introduction to a new foster home.

Drop-in service

A potential side-effect of this model noted by staff was that of dependency of the young people. Staff felt that it was sometimes possible that the level of support offered by the drop-in could discourage young people from developing other networks of support in the community.

Street-based work

One concern expressed by staff involved in street-based work was the possibility that their support made it easier for young people to remain in risky situations on the street, rather than seeking a way out.

Effects relevant to more than one model

Effects of a disclosure of abuse

Staff in several of the projects voiced concern about the possible effects resulting from dealing with a disclosure of abuse by a young person. The positive effects for the young person can be to unburden something that has been troubling them for some time, and to escape from further abuse. However, staff felt some misgivings about the outcomes of a disclosure for a young person once the information resulted in child protection procedures being instigated. These misgivings were in relation either to the young person experiencing rejection by their family, or disbelief from statutory agencies, or simply being swept along by a process over which they had no control:

> *"If young people make a disclosure we may need to start child protection proceedings. We offer to be there with them, but the system takes over and we get lost during the process. I'm not sure if it's negative but it feels like we've broken a promise."*

Facilitating running away?

A concern raised both by staff within the projects and a number of other professionals was the possibility that the projects may facilitate or even encourage young people running away or being on the streets. There was a belief amongst the staff at Leeds Safe House and amongst social workers and residential care staff, that a minority of young people, especially those living in residential care, may run to the refuge, rather than away from where they were living.

For example, some young people were going to the refuge because they preferred the regime there to that in their children's home. Whilst it is true that a young person doing this is making a positive choice, it was seen by staff and other professionals as being a 'misuse' of refuge and as taking up a bed space that might have been needed by another young person at risk. To a limited extent, the same issue appears to have come up in the Porth Project, although again we must note that the project is at an early stage of its development.

Similar issues came up in the two street-based projects. Street-based staff were concerned that their presence could encourage young people to be on the streets. This was also a concern of an external professional:

> *"Young people have been leaving a specific children's home, encouraged to return to the city centre for freebies. A safe, friendly, reliable face in the city centre encourages them to run."*

Some grounds for this concern were also provided by two young people who said that they came in to Manchester city centre to maintain contact with Safe in the City.

EFFECTS ON PROJECT STAFF

The innovative nature of the projects, and the extreme situations of many of the young people with whom the projects work, have considerable effects on staff. Most of the staff, and the refuge carers in South Wales, were willing to comment on how the work had affected them as individuals.

Positive aspects

There had been a number of positive aspects of the experience of working in the projects for staff and carers. For example:

- The development of new skills:

  "It has given me the opportunity to change my ways of communicating with young people by giving them control of the way they go forward. It's been very important to me."

- A greater understanding of young people and the issues that affect them, and elements of personal growth:

  "It's opened my eyes. I was shocked at first. It's made me a lot more tolerant about various groups."

- A feeling of value and worth in the work that is achieved:

  "Elated if a young person is speaking out in a meeting. It means I'm filled with hope."

Negative aspects

However, there were several common negative themes amongst people's comments:

- Anger at the injustices young people face and frustration at the small amount of change that is often achieved:

  "It's made me realise more how unfairly young people are treated as a whole. Sometimes I feel despairing that there is nothing to effect real change, or meet the long-term needs of young people."

- The emotionally draining nature of the work:

  "I know that the work drains my physical and emotional energy and saps my self-confidence. Sometimes when I come home I feel like a zombie."

  "It's painful to walk away from young people on the streets. It's difficult to live with some of the decisions they make."

- High stress levels in all the projects, stemming from different factors according to the setting. The stresses for street-based workers include working in situations in which they are vulnerable to threats of violence, the unhealthy environment, and the difficulty of getting immediate back-up support:

  "There are dangers to staff and young people. We live with the risks that young people experience .... Staff are open to physical threats, guns, etc. .... It's cold and wet."

For refuge-based staff the stresses arise from the 24-hour nature of the service and from the pressure of working intensively for short periods of time with a rapid turnover of young people:

"The 24-hour service model is too intrusive into people's lives — the pressures on staff and the physical demands. It feels like the job is risky."

and (for Leeds Safe House) from the need to exercise some control when young people are living in a residential setting:

"I'm not sure it's right for us to have to expect to be battered [emotionally] by young people, and I think that's what they do."

Whilst most 'social work' jobs entail some or all of the above stresses, it does seem that the streetwork projects are involved in a particularly high-risk area of work, which can take its toll on the staff employed within them. The above comments are not just applicable to project workers and refuge carers involved in the direct day-to-day work with young people, but also to managers, administrative workers and other support staff who work in the same environment.

EFFECTS ON OTHER PEOPLE AND ORGANISATIONS

The projects' work may have unanticipated effects on other people or organisations.

Positive effects on practice

Some professionals in other agencies identified positive effects of the projects' work on their own practice. For example:

> *"For the child in crisis they are very warm, caring people who give the child a listening ear. They had the ability to see where the child is coming from, probably more so than I was able to. I found that helpful to me."*

> *"They set up meetings to help them* [young people] *express their views. I think that's good because it's not just talking. We can all get together and look at the problems."*

Effects on parents

However, some external professionals expressed concerns about perceived effects of the projects' work. Three social workers felt that the work of refuge-based services could have unproductive effects on parents:

> *"It can 'depower' parents. It can have a long-term effect on working on parenting skills."*

> *"It can make parents feel extremely disempowered. They were not allowed to know where their daughter was or what was happening. In the mother's mind they harboured her daughter for a fortnight and then put her back on the streets."*

Effects on the relationship between young people and professionals

There were also possible effects on the relationship between young people and key professionals:

> *"It doesn't help a relationship if you know workers in an agency have a negative view of social workers. I don't think it helped her, and it didn't help our work with her."*

SUMMARY

As has already been discussed in Chapter 9, the projects' work with young people may lead to a number of positive outcomes for the young people themselves, for the project and its staff, and for the other adults and networks with whom the young people and the projects have contact. Nevertheless, as in any area of work which is focused on one-to-one contact with, and advocacy for, individuals — and particularly with those who are young, vulnerable and at a time of crisis — the work of the projects is inherently 'risky' and there are a number of potential side-effects.

For young people, these effects may be very positive — such as friendships with others going through similar experiences. However, they may also, potentially, be negative — such as being introduced to negative forms of behaviour by peers, or developing an over-dependency on the support offered by the projects.

Staff may enjoy the feeling of value and worth which their work can offer, but also become emotionally and physically drained by the stress that the work involves.

Professionals in other agencies and parents may welcome the intervention of the projects as a means of helping them to begin rebuilding their relationship with a young person, or at least of offering them the relative comfort of knowing that the young person has support from responsible and caring professionals. On the other hand, some may resent that same intervention, seeing it as an unwelcome intrusion into their relationship or work with a young person.

In the next chapter we examine in more detail some of the other issues raised by the work of the projects. We note also the implications and effects these have on the projects themselves, on the young people and the agencies they work with, and on the future development of this area of expertise.

CHAPTER 11
Other Issues Regarding the Projects' Work

ACCESSIBILITY TO YOUNG PEOPLE

As has already been described, each project offers an individual range of services which are targeted at particular groups of young people. The two street-based projects focus their work primarily on the city centre, whereas the two refuge-based projects accept referrals from a wider geographical area. The first approach is thus focused on working intensively with a specific group of young people, whilst the second offers a more limited opportunity of access to a wider group of young people. There are therefore differences in the way various young people experience the accessibility of each of the projects.

It would seem from the comparison of young people in contact with the projects presented in Chapter 8, that refuge-based projects are used by a wider range of young people, including young people who have not run away many times and young people who have never spent extended periods of time on the streets. To a lesser extent, a drop-in service will also be accessible to these young people.

On the other hand, the street-based projects are directly accessible to young people face to face. This may be an advantage compared to the refuge-based projects, where the first point of contact is the telephone which may be a barrier to some young people (see below).

The other key difference between the projects is their accessibility at different times of the day. The two refuge-based services are accessible to young people by telephone 24 hours a day, whereas the two street-based projects are only accessible for parts of the day and evening on certain days of the week.

ANTI-DISCRIMINATORY ISSUES

All projects strive to provide an anti-discriminatory service to young people in their area. There is evidence that Youth Link has been successful in engaging with young gay men, and that Leeds Safe House, Safe in the City and the Porth Project are working with young people from ethnic minority populations (Chapter 8).

There are, however, concerns that the projects may not be equally accessible to all groups of young people due to a variety of factors.

In terms of ethnic minority populations, these considerations are closely linked with the need to understand the issue of being away from home from a range of cultural perspectives. Previous research (Abrahams and Mungall, 1992; Rees, 1993) has found a significantly higher incidence of running away amongst young people of African-Caribbean origin than amongst white young people. However, these studies were not able to compare the significance of running away or the running away experiences of these two groups of young people. Little is therefore currently known about how (if at all) the needs of African-Caribbean young people who run away may differ from those of white young people. For example, some groups of black young people may not go to the city centre when they run away, and thus a city centre-based project would tend not to work with them. Similarly, a refuge may be perceived by black young people as not being geared towards their needs.

As noted earlier (page 101), one particular concern of staff at Leeds Safe House has been the potential effects on Asian young women of a stay in refuge. There was a feeling that since running away can be a particularly difficult thing for them to do, it may be better to offer them the option of receiving support from staff outside the refuge.

A research study carried out by The Children's Society into homelessness and running away amongst young black people in Newport has indicated the need to approach this issue without pre-conceptions or stereotypes:

> *"Many workers assumed that the research was about young Asian women escaping from arranged marriages and domineering males. For some young Asian women that might be the reality. But again, workers should not presume, as many in the sample have done, that all Asian young women will be running to avoid arranged marriages. There were wider cultural issues for these young women to consider but none of the young women who were interviewed were fleeing arranged marriages. Like many other young women in general, the young black women interviewed were running because of physical violence, emotional and sexual abuse and other family conflicts."* (Patel, 1994: page 35)

Leeds Safe House has also come to recognise the need to develop better community links with ethnic minority communities in order to promote understanding of the project's work.

Staff at all the projects have also commented about the need to consider the issue of disability and how this may have a bearing both on running away and on the projects' accessibility. For example, it may be that many young people with limited mobility are living in abusive situations but are unable to express their unhappiness by leaving. Similarly, the fact that the refuge-based projects are only able to be contacted by telephone may be a barrier to deaf young people referring themselves.

Finally, staff were concerned that organisational policy means that they are unable to offer young people the option of refuge with lesbian and gay foster carers.

A 'YOUNG PERSON-CENTRED' APPROACH

All projects are committed to the concept of working with young people in a 'young person-centred' way. This involves, for example, listening to young people and taking what they say seriously, involving them in all decision-making processes, operating a system of open records, and actively promoting the views of the young person. This approach allows project workers to engage young people, including the most marginalised (see Chapter 9), and provides a coherent frame of reference for practice and policy.

However, this approach differs from that taken by many statutory agencies and was often mentioned by professionals in other agencies as a source of conflict between them and the projects. It is also an issue which came up regularly in the interviews with project staff, both as a perceived strength in the way the projects worked, and as something which many felt needed further clarification:

> "A young person-centred approach is good for listening and working out something to do for young people. But I think it's an ideal .... I'd like somebody to tell me what it means, to define it. I see it as that the young person is the focus of what you do, which is fine. But if it means doing everything the young person wanted or said, I don't think you can do it. I think we tried that at the start and it knackered everybody and damaged our relationship with other agencies." (project worker)

This highlights some key questions: Does a 'young person-centred' approach mean maintaining that young people have an absolute right to self-determination, and that workers have to support them in that? Do workers have any responsibilities to protect young people? Two quotes from different workers in the same project illustrate the dilemma:

> "[There are] *real instances where you want to lead it and take it away from the young person, as an adult, but we have to work at the young person's pace and let them make mistakes.*"

> "*Young people's rights are taken too far sometimes and we have failed to protect them ... drugs, prostitution ... we haven't changed their lives. Do they have that right to press the self-destruct button?*"

Confidentiality and open records

Policy regarding confidentiality inevitably has a direct bearing on the work of the projects and has been a subject of considerable debate among project staff. As the following quotes illustrate, the issues are complex and there is no unified view:

> "*The confidentiality policy has meant that it has worked against some young people who have either left or not come in. These young people had also felt closed down by statutory child protection agencies. I've shifted my position. I think a project like this should be brave enough to offer 100% confidentiality.*"

> "*I've always held that to promise kids total confidentiality is a mistake ... I don't think you can turn a blind eye if a young person is going back to an abusive situation. You shouldn't promise something you can't deliver.*"

Another issue of debate in a 'young-person centred' approach is the question of how much use should be made of other people's opinions about a young person: are other adults' views on young people always 'value judgements'; or are they useful to working with a young person?

It should be pointed out that the projects do not refuse information from other professionals. However, the projects' policy that all information is open to young people can mean that in some cases staff from other agencies are unwilling to provide information. In addition, a number felt that work could have been achieved more quickly with more exchange of information.

Advocacy roles

Another aspect of a 'young person-centred' approach is the advocacy role which the projects adopt. Again, this was the subject of much debate within the projects:

> *"Social services see us as a rather unprofessional organisation, that we collude with young people, that we work from misconceptions, and therefore that we work against the interests of young people. It might happen, but we are advocates, we speak on their behalf."*

> *"Advocacy is certainly something we should be doing. However, successful advocacy is not simply making statutory agencies as uncomfortable as possible and presenting young people's wishes irrespective of 'achievability' or 'rightness'. You can't advocate without a clear sense of your own and your organisation's values or if you don't respect other agencies."*

Amongst professionals in other agencies, the issue of advocacy styles elicited even more comments than the issue of confidentiality and appeared in some cases to be a major source of conflict. Some professionals (especially social workers) felt personally attacked by project staff undertaking advocacy, which had inevitably damaged relationships between the project and agencies. Some also felt that the advocacy style had damaged relationships with parents.

> *"We felt rubbished by the project staff. They were listening totally to the young person whereas we have to be more balanced. I'm not against this approach but it's bound to create strain."*

There were also a number of comments about the projects raising young people's expectations, giving them the impression that they have "idealistic rights which legally they don't have". For example:

> *"[They] encouraged her to ask for the right to live independently when she was pregnant, 14 and on a care order. She was expecting to get rights that she wasn't going to get. I don't mind expectations being raised if they can be achieved, but not if we, and foster carers, have to pick up the pieces after."* (social worker)

This issue is also recognised by project staff as a source of potential difficulty:

> *"It's a dilemma arguing for something the young person has identified which you don't think is achievable. You might disagree, but you are there to work with them. The outcome is not the only thing, it's about being heard."*

Finally, there is a fundamental issue about whether the outcomes young people want are necessarily in their best interests:

> *"There are young people who are dying to go into care, and the project fights for their rights to go into care. They go in, then a couple of months later it's horrible and then they refer to the project again and again …. Some young people, all they want at first is to leave home, then later all they want is to go back …. Is fighting for a place in care the right thing to do?"*

The above discussion has, of necessity, only briefly covered some of the main areas of debate about the projects' processes of working with young people. These areas are part of a much wider debate about young people's rights and responsibilities at various ages; about professionally defined needs and the status of professionals' perceptions; and about young people's role in society.

RELATIONSHIPS WITH OTHER AGENCIES

Given the material of the previous section, which highlighted a fundamental difference of perspectives and an element of conflict between the projects and statutory agencies, it is not surprising that the projects' relationships with other agencies have been mixed.

Relationships with social services departments, for example, have been problematic. Even where projects have had a positive relationship at a senior management level, there seems to have been a fair amount of conflict at a practice level.

On the other hand, the projects' relationships with the police have generally been good. In fact, from interviews with key personnel in the local police forces, the two refuge-based projects appear to have built up excellent relationships with the police, who recognise the need for refuge for some young people and have been significant supporters of the projects. Any difficulties which have arisen seem to have been overcome by discussion and co-operation.

PROJECT DEVELOPMENT

In an area of innovative work, it is inevitable that there will be many debates about its future development. A general theme across all four projects is a wish to develop advocacy work. Other major issues were reflected in interviews with staff and illustrate some of the ways in which each project is attempting to ensure that it can best meet the needs of its own target group of young people.

Safe in the City

In Safe in the City a major issue is whether the project should now persist in its original plan of providing refuge through refuge carers. There seems to be a general feeling amongst the staff team that there are too many drawbacks and that, in any case, most of the young people with whom the project had contact were very resourceful in finding somewhere to stay themselves:

> *"Refuge as in Section 51 is constrained by regulation, it's become insti-tutionalised .... It would distort us. You have to compromise to get a certificate .... It also has high resource demands within a finite pot and takes away from other areas."*

There is also a debate about whether the project should have a base where young people can come.

Youth Link

Youth Link is debating whether there is a need for a refuge service in Birmingham and whether this would be the best use of resources.

Another issue for staff is the balance between the drop-in and street-based elements of the service. These are generally seen as complementing each other, but some people expressed concern that when resources are stretched, it is more likely that the street-based work is reduced.

> *"If you provide drop-in at certain times, you have to keep it going, detached work gets dropped, but young people expect that to happen and if you don't do it for a few weeks it's very hard to go back into it, you lose continuity."*

Leeds Safe House

In Leeds there are concerns about whether the young people who use the refuge always needed it and whether the project is reaching the people at whom it is aimed. There is also a recognition that provision of refuge can be extremely labour-intensive and that the requirements of Section 51 certification are making the provision more bureaucratic.

Whilst there is a general commitment to the continued provision of refuge in one form or another, there is a large majority feeling that the project should distinguish between the services it offers:

> *"I think it is difficult to combine our advocacy/'move-on' role with our residential provision. I think lots of confusion/clashes stem from the attempted co-existence of these two quite disparate needs."*

The Porth Project

Porth is at a much earlier stage of its development. However, some of the debates in Leeds are reflected in the project, particularly whether young people always need refuge, and whether it may be possible to separate provision of refuge from advocacy:

> *"An advice and information service would open up the service to many more young people. They might need a worker to support them in a change of placement, but might be OK where they are. At the moment you get refuge and advocacy — you can't have the one without the other."*

SUMMARY

The work of the projects reflects many of the issues and dilemmas faced by anyone offering a direct service to young people: whether the service is accessible to all those who need it; how best to ensure that the service provided caters for the needs of all young people, whatever their race, culture, gender, sexuality, or disability; and the working policies and practices that need to be developed in order to work most effectively and most fairly with young people.

SECTION 3

IMPLICATIONS OF THE
RESEARCH FINDINGS

CHAPTER 12
A Model of Intervention

The research has indicated the diverse nature of young people who may be described as 'running away' and the diverse needs these young people have. In Section 1 we presented a model of running away 'pathways' derived from the data (Figure 6.3, page 63). Comparison of information about young people in contact with each of the projects within The Children's Society's streetwork programme (Chapter 8) suggested that all the projects work predominantly with young people who are already some way along these pathways. The projects offer a model of intervention specifically focused on a small but highly vulnerable group of young people who have run frequently from their families and from substitute care. Some have become detached from family and care.

Yet the diversity of the running away 'pathways' outlined in the model suggests that a range of interventions are required in order to meet the needs of all young people who run away from where they live. For example, 'pathway 1' — running away once or twice and then ceasing to run away — is by far the numerically largest subgroup of young people who run away. Whilst refuge-based services are more likely than street-based services to work with young people in this group, it remains the case that relatively few of these young people use refuge services. It is possible therefore that these young people have needs which are not fully met by the existing models in the streetwork programme. It also seems that the projects have very limited contact with young people before they start running away, and do not generally do preventative work with young people who may run away. Using the concepts of primary, secondary and tertiary intervention, some practical initiatives are suggested overleaf.

Figure 12.1 A Model of Intervention

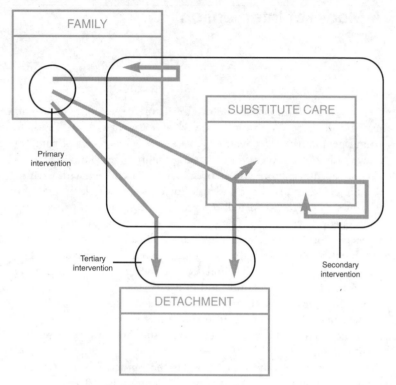

PRIMARY INTERVENTION

Primary intervention focuses on preventative work with all young people and their families within the community. This could take the form, for example, of education projects such as the consideration of issues around running away as part of the personal and social education carried out in schools, and the promotion of the education for citizenship cross-curricular theme within schools. 'The family' is central to the process of becoming an adult in our society, in terms of preparation and support. Preparation for becoming a parent is therefore another important element of primary intervention.[1]

In addition, primary intervention needs to address family policy in general: policy that encourages families to make children their central concern and that allows the voice of the child to be listened to

---

[1] The Children's Society publishes resource packs and other material aimed at teachers and others working with young people addressing these particular topics, e.g. *Education for Citizenship* (1991) and *Education for Parenthood* (1994).

and valued, may result in making the family a more 'child-centred' environment.

SECONDARY INTERVENTION

Secondary intervention should focus on support to young people who have run away once or twice, usually from their families (Pathway 1 above), and also on young people who are at the early stages of running away from care settings (Pathway 2). These are clearly young people in need.

Interventions would have to engage young people in settings other than their home environments, such as schools or youth clubs, in order to reach those who have run away or who are considering running away again. Such work could offer young people opportunities to discuss alternative solutions and support in working towards the resolution of problems. A telephone helpline specifically targeted at those who are thinking about running away may be one form of service that could be integrated into other existing service models.

A 'mediation service' could be provided, which would help negotiate the return of a young person to the family home and would offer assistance to the family in addressing some of the issues that precipitated the running away episode. Part III Section 17 of the Children Act 1989 requires local authorities to offer services to children in need, and this service could be facilitated through joint working strategies between the police, local authorities and voluntary organisations. Such a service could be a valuable addition to current service provision and contribute to young people not following the pathways to detachment.

Further secondary intervention should be focused on the provision of substitute care. Just as attempts to improve the quality of life in families could contribute to the prevention of running away, so improving the quality of life in substitute care may prevent young people running again and for longer. Strategies to improve resourcing, service delivery and staff training would have a general impact; more targeted programmes addressing the reintegration of runaways into substitute care settings could have a similarly beneficial effect. These issues are discussed further, in terms of social policy, on pages 122-123.

TERTIARY INTERVENTION

As discussed above, various models of tertiary intervention are already in operation as part of The Children's Society's programme of streetwork. These interventions aim to provide contact, refuge, advocacy and, if possible, to negotiate a return to substitute care or family settings.

The information we have collected suggests that careful research is required in the development of tertiary intervention models. Whilst a city centre street-based detached model has proved to be appropriate for large cities such as Birmingham and Manchester, it is dependent on the existence of an identifiable area where young people congregate on the streets. Information gathered in Leeds, for example, suggests that there is no 'street culture' of young people in the city centre there, and this may also be true of other smaller cities and towns. It is possible, therefore, that a more dispersed detached model would be more appropriate in some areas, or that a completely different model of service provision would be required. Thus, whilst general models of primary and secondary intervention are likely to be appropriate for most areas, a tertiary intervention model needs to be developed with a particular attention to local circumstances.

The Area Child Protection Committees (ACPCs), which exist in every local authority area, are in an excellent strategic position to co-ordinate creative agency responses to young people on the streets. The ACPCs include representation from social services, education, housing, health, police and, sometimes, voluntary organisations, all of which are crucial to providing services for young people on the streets. The ACPC, therefore, is potentially a forum which could co-ordinate services to young people who, as has we have already shown, are often estranged from the provision of basic services.

CHAPTER 13
Social Policy Issues

Our research has highlighted a number of broader social policy issues relevant to the young people with whom the streetwork projects work.

THE POSITION OF YOUNG PEOPLE UNDER 16 LIVING AWAY FROM BOTH FAMILY AND SUBSTITUTE CARE

In both our questionnaire and interview samples we found young people under 16 living away from both their families and any form of substitute care; some of them had already been doing so for more than six months. In strict legal terms this should not be possible: any young person under 16 should either be living with someone who has parental responsibility or be provided with accommodation by the local authority under Section 20 of the Children Act 1989. Any young person considered to be 'in need' should also be in receipt of services under Part III of the Children Act.

The young people in our samples, therefore, found themselves in a service 'vacuum': they had nowhere to live; they had no obvious source of income; they were not attending school; and often lacked any link into state services or the adult world. We can see such people as 'marginalised' or 'detached' from the adult world. They are 'non-citizens', living independently but unable to claim the rights or exercise the responsibilities which most adults take for granted.

Many of the young people will have presented a major challenge to their families and the care system and will have been seen as unco-operative or uncontrollable. Many will have brought disadvantage with them, and then have continued to accumulate disadvantage during their years of detachment. This study could not track the long-term outcomes for such young people, but it seems certain that they would find re-integration into social institutions difficult.

The young people we spoke to often only had one link into the adult world: the streetwork projects. The work of the projects in this area then is invaluable. It also raises the question, however, of how young people in areas of the country not covered by similar projects are able to make any links into the adult world at all.

THE CRIMINALISATION OF YOUNG PEOPLE INVOLVED IN PROSTITUTION

The issue of young people providing sex for money as a means of survival came across powerfully in the information we gathered from young people and professionals. This is an issue of particular concern, as many young people will have experienced the abuse of power within their birth families and are then exposed to the abuse of adult male power on the streets in order to survive.

Young people who are sexually abused by adults in family settings may well be subject to a child protection investigation under Section 47 of the Children Act. Yet some young people in the research samples who were aged under 16 had been cautioned by the police following involvement in prostitution. They have thus been criminalised. This situation appears highly unjust: young people abused in family settings are seen as victims, whereas those of the same age who are involved in street activities are labelled as criminals.

THE QUALITY OF LIFE FOR YOUNG PEOPLE IN SUBSTITUTE CARE

As we have seen, many of the young people reported negative experiences of their lives in both residential and foster care. Some young people identified these negative experiences as a reason for them running away or being forced to leave. In our model of running away pathways we have identified, as a form of secondary intervention, measures to improve the quality of life for young people in substitute care. Such interventions could be based on:

(a) Recognising the importance of residential care for older young people. Despite the overall increase in the use of foster care, residential care remains a crucial resource, particularly for older young people (Biehal et al., 1992).

(b) The adoption of a strategic approach to family support, residential and foster care. Substitute care needs to be seen as a positive service with a clear location within the continuum of child and family services.

(c) Carers need to develop clear strategies for working with young people who have run away. Factors which facilitate the successful reintegration of the young person into the care setting need to be identified and developed.

(d) The young people we interviewed often spoke of physical intimidation from other young people in residential care settings and identified this as a factor precipitating their running away. Addressing this issue presents a major challenge for the residential care system.

THE LEVEL OF SUPPORT PROVIDED TO YOUNG PEOPLE LEAVING CARE

Previous research specifically examining leaving-care issues (Stein and Carey, 1985; Biehal et al., 1992) has identified a problem of young people leaving local authority accommodation being offered variable levels of support — both emotional and material.

In both our interview and questionnaire samples we found young people over 16 who qualify for 'advice and assistance' under Section 24 of the Children Act but reported having little contact with social workers and having received no practical assistance. Such young people seem to have accumulated disadvantage, first through their early family experiences and subsequently through their in-care experience. This is then in danger of being replicated in the post-16 phase. Local authorities need urgently to address the issue of support to such care leavers, particularly those who may have been challenging during their care careers and later become detached from the care system.

THE IMPACT OF FAMILY BREAKDOWN ON YOUNG PEOPLE

As we have seen, many young people in the sample had experienced family breakdown, separation from one or both parents and had lived in reconstituted families. This often led to difficult relationships with their birth parents or parents' new partners. The most negative of these experiences included extreme forms of violence and abuse.

This evidence should not be used to suggest that it is impossible to reconstitute families successfully. The young people in contact with the projects are those who have had negative experiences and are not necessarily representative of the population as a whole, although earlier research (Rees, 1993) found that the rate of running away was significantly higher amongst young people living with a parent and step-parent than amongst young people living with both birth parents or with a lone parent.

As increasing numbers of young people experience family breakdown (National Children's Bureau, 1993) this raises a serious issue of the impact this process has on them. How can we ensure that young people's needs are met when adults are in conflict? How can we make sure that the voices of young people are heard? Conciliation and mediation services, for example, offer parents who are experiencing marital breakdown counselling and advice on how to work together to put their children's interests first. They have achieved considerable success in reducing levels of conflict and stress. Extension of these services to all separating couples who require them would help protect the welfare of children and young people.

THE POTENTIAL LINKS BETWEEN RUNNING AWAY AND HOMELESSNESS

The majority of young people over 16 in the interview sample had experienced periods of homelessness since the age of 16. This fact in itself does not constitute proof of a link between running away and homelessness. However, in view of the detachment and marginalisation that many of the young people have experienced before the age of 16, it would not be surprising if such a link does exist. Research carried out in the USA found a link between regular running away under 16 and later youth homelessness (Simons and Whitbeck, 1991).

It is notable that the young people we interviewed often expressed reluctance to use hostels and night shelters for homeless people as an intermediate step on the road to permanent housing, mainly because of the rules that these services operated. On the other hand, they often felt that they would need support in establishing themselves in independent accommodation. This therefore presents a challenge for housing agencies: to offer a route which is acceptable to young people who have become 'detached' by which they can gain access to permanent housing.

EDUCATIONAL ISSUES

The data presented in Section 1 of this report revealed that few of the young people were still engaged in the education system, and that some young people had become permanently detached from it at as young as 13 years old. Young people often felt that there was little point in their re-entering the education system after a period of detachment. The relationship between running away and educational detachment is reinforced by other research which found a link between young people running away and regular truancy from school (Rees, 1993).

There is evidence therefore that young people who run away regularly are in danger of accumulating educational disadvantage in addition to other disadvantages. It is ironic that young people for whom the local authority often has parental responsibility are marginalised from the educational services provided by that authority. It appears that here again there is a need to create routes through which young people who have become 'detached' can be reintegrated into the educational system.

THE NEED TO DEVELOP A CO-ORDINATED RESPONSE

Currently, young people who run away are often returned to the place they ran from as a matter of course. It is evident from the data presented in this report that many young people have strong motivations for leaving home or substitute care. One way of addressing this and ensuring the welfare of the young person would be to develop a series of local services which are immediately available to these young people, and which give them the opportunity to discuss the issues that have led them to run away and to explore possible alternative solutions to their situation. Such services would have to be demonstrably independent of the statutory services whilst working in partnership with them. There is a need to pilot and evaluate services of this kind.

CHAPTER 14
Concluding Remarks

The streetwork projects outlined and evaluated by this research are working with a small but highly vulnerable group of young people. They are a group who run away regularly from their families and from substitute care. Some have become completely detached from their family or care.

The average age for young men to leave the parental home is about 22, whilst for young women it is about 20 (Jones, 1987). And yet the streetwork projects are working with under-16-year-olds, some of whom have already lived for more than six months detached from their families. In their short lives they have experienced high levels of disruption, including family breakdown, conflict and abuse. Most have also spent periods in substitute care. But they have rarely achieved the stability previously lacking in their lives and some of these young people run regularly from care. Perhaps not surprisingly, few of these young people attend school regularly or are able to trust or depend upon adults.

'Running away' can be viewed as a positive act: getting out of an abusive family situation rather than, *in extremis*, taking one's own life or persistent self-harm. Or it could be seen as an act of assertion in what is perceived to be a situation in which a young person has no power over their lives: "nobody cares about me, nobody gives a damn". Most young people run *from* somebody or something rather than *to* something or somebody else, and most young people do not feel that running away resolved their initial problems. In their experience of running away, young people are often both 'victim' and 'villain': fear, loneliness and being assaulted combine with stealing, begging or sex for money in order to survive 'on the streets'. Perhaps only by linking these two dimensions will we recognise the heavy demands placed on streetwork and related projects, and the complexity of child protection issues.

The main purpose of the streetwork programme is to assist these young people: the refuge-based projects intervening in the earlier stages of young people running from family and substitute care, and the street-based projects mainly working with 'detached' young people. The projects commonly achieve positive outcomes in relation to meeting young people's immediate needs, establishing positive relationships with marginalised young people, and facilitating change in young people's lives.

In terms of the future development of the projects, the research has highlighted differences between their accessibility to white and to black young people, and to able-bodied and disabled young people. There are also differences in accessibility between refuge-based and street-based projects. The 'young person-centred' approach adopted by all the projects raised a number of issues, including confidentiality and open records, and the role of advocacy work.

A number of key areas have been identified for consideration by agencies working with young people. These include the current provision of residential care, educational support, and the need for a co-ordinated response to working with young people.

The key social policy issues include the position of young people under 16 living away from family and substitute care, the criminalisation of young people involved in prostitution, the quality of life for young people in substitute care, and the impact of family breakdown on young people.

The research represents a challenge not only to those agencies working directly with young people, but to society as a whole. For simultaneously we need to encourage young people not to run away in the first place, through early support to them and to families in difficulty, and we need to respond to the vulnerable group of young people who do run away. The former demands a primary prevention programme including 'running away issues' as part of the personal and social education curriculum, parenting preparation, and the development of more positive attitudes towards young people in society. The latter, secondary and tertiary prevention, demands a well co-ordinated response aimed at working with young people and families and improving the quality of substitute care, so that no young people under 16 will find themselves 'on the streets'.

APPENDIX
Comparison with Research in other Countries

The research findings presented in Chapters 3 and 4 are similar in many respects to research on 'running away' and 'street children' which has been undertaken in other countries, particularly the USA. A brief summary of some of these findings is presented below.

Running away experiences

A study by Brennan et al. (1978) in the USA produced similar findings to recent survey research in the UK. Their findings suggest a significant incidence of running away (one in nine young people in a large survey). About half of runaways ran alone; around three-quarters left home only once; half of the runaways returned home within three days; half of the runaways travelled less than ten miles. These findings are broadly consistent with those in a survey carried out in Leeds (Rees, 1993). Similarly, the fact that only 38% of parents of runaways reported the incident to the police, and that most runaways returned home of their own volition, fits in with current knowledge about runaways in the UK.

Several studies, including Shane (1989), found that many homeless and runaway young people had been forced to leave home rather than run away.

Whitbeck and Simons (1990) examined the victimisation of young runaways on the streets. They found different experiences for males and females. Females were most likely to be sexually assaulted (42% of a sample had been), whereas males were more likely to be threatened or assaulted with a weapon. They found a link between running away and 'deviant' subsistence strategies, and then a strong link between these strategies and victimisation.

Cohen, MacKenzie and Yates (1991) found that one-quarter of homeless young people/runaways were providing sex for money in order to survive, compared to 0.3% of non-homeless teenagers. Homeless young people and runaways were six times more likely to be at risk of HIV infection than other young people.

Family background

A number of studies (e.g. Farber (1984)) found significantly higher levels of physical violence in the families of runaways than in those of non-runaways. Whitbeck and Simons and Janus et al. (1987) both found that the population of runaways had experienced much higher rates of physical and sexual abuse than did randomly sampled populations of young people.

Brennan et al. found a number of aspects of family relationships which are significantly more common for runaways than non-runaways, including physical violence, marital conflict, parental remoteness from the child, and negative labelling by parents. Johnson and Carter (1980) state that runaways' families "are typically marred by high rates of internal conflict, divorce, residential mobility and death". Both Brennan et al. and Ek and Steelman (1988) found that differential treatment of siblings was a significant factor in the family situation of runaways. Roberts (1982) found a significant level of alcohol-related problems in parents of runaways.

In one respect, US findings differ from research findings in the UK. Shane (1989) found that young people living in single parent families are significantly more likely to run away than other young people. However, the research presented in this report, and in Rees (1993), suggests that in the UK the highest rates of running away are from reconstituted families, whilst running away rates from single parent families are similar to those from families with both birth parents.

School experience

Brennan et al. found significant differences between runaways and non-runaways in terms of experiences of school. Runaways, for example, had less positive attitudes to school. They were also twice as likely as non-runaways to truant, to be beaten by teachers, and to be suspended or expelled from school.

Cohen et al. found that 38% of a sample of homeless young people/runaways had dropped out of school compared to 7% of a comparison group of non-homeless young people.

Self-harm and depression

Cohen et al. found that homeless young people/runaways were far more likely to be depressed and actively suicidal than non-homeless young people. They found no evidence, however, that they were more likely to have major mental health problems.

Drug and substance use

Cohen et al. found that homeless young people/runaways had considerably more experience with drugs than other young people — 54% had used marijuana, 35% stimulants, and 8% had injected drugs — although few of them felt they had a drug problem.

Long-term effects of running away

Relatively little research has been done into this area. However, Simons and Whitbeck (1991) looked at the possibility that running away during adolescence is a precursor to adult homelessness. They found empirical support for their hypothesis that many young people who run away repeatedly and for considerable lengths of time grow up to become homeless adults.

REFERENCES

Abrahams, C. and Mungall, R. *Runaways: Exploding the Myths.* NCH - Action for Children, 1992.

Akland, J. 'Institutional Reactions to Absconding' in *British Journal Of Social Work,* volume II, pages 171–187, 1981.

Berry, J. *Daily Experience in Residential Life.* Routledge and Kegan Paul, 1975.

Biehal, N., Clayden, J., Stein, M. and Wade, J. *Prepared for Living? a survey of young people leaving the care of three local authorities.* National Children's Bureau, 1992.

Brennan, T, Huizinga, D. and Elliott, D. *The Social Psychology of Runaways.* Lexington Books, 1978.

Bullock, R., Little, M. and Milham, S. *Residential Care for Children: a review of the research.* HMSO, 1993.

Cliffe, D. and Berridge, D. *Closing Children's Homes.* National Children's Bureau, 1991.

Cohen, E., MacKenzie and Yates. 'A psychological risk assessment instrument - implications for designing effective intervention programs for runaway youth' in *Journal of Adolescent Health,* volume 12 (7), pages 539-544, 1991.

Ek, C.A. and Steelman. 'Becoming a runaway - from the accounts of youthful runners' in *Youth and Society,* volume 19 (3), pages 334-358, 1988.

Farber, E.D. 'Violence in families of adolescent runaways' in *Child Abuse and Neglect,* volume 8 (3), pages 295-299, 1984.

Janus, M. et al. *Adolescent Runaways: Causes and Consequences.* Lexington Books, 1987.

Johnson, R. and Carter. 'Flight of the young - why children run away from their homes' in *Adolescence,* volume 15, pages 483-489, 1980.

132

Jones, G. 'Leaving the Parental Home' in *Journal of Social Policy,* volume 16 (1), pages 40-74, 1987.

Milham, S., Bullock, R. and Chernett, P. *After Grace - Teeth.* Human Context Books, 1975.

Milham, S., Bullock, R., Hosie, K. and Haak, M. *Lost in Care.* Gower Publishing Co. Ltd, 1986.

National Children's Bureau. *Children in Danger.* NCB, 1993.

Newman, C. *Young Runaways: findings from Britain's first safe house.* The Children's Society, 1989.

Page, R. and Clark, G.A. *Who Cares? Young People in Care Speak Out.* National Children's Bureau, 1977.

Patel, G. *The Porth Project: a study of homelessness and running away amongst young black people in Newport, Gwent.* The Children's Society, 1994.

Rees, G. *Hidden Truths: young people's experiences of running away.* The Children's Society, 1993.

Roberts, A.R. 'Adolescent runaways in suburbia - a new typology' in *Adolescence,* volume 17 (6), pages 387-396, 1982.

Rowe, J., Hundleby, M. and Garnett, L. *Child Care Now.* British Agencies for Adoption and Fostering, 1989.

Shane, P.G. 'Changing patterns among homeless and runaway youth' in *American Journal of Orthopsychiatry,* volume 59 (2), pages 208-214, 1989.

Simons, R.L. and Whitbeck, L.B. 'Running away during adolescence as a precursor to adult homelessness' in *Social Services Review,* volume 65 (2), pages 224-247, June 1991.

Stein, M. 'The Abuses and Uses of Residential Care' in Ferguson et al. (eds) *Surviving Childhood Adversity.* Dublin, 1993.

Stein, M. and Carey, K. *Leaving Care.* Blackwell Publishers, 1985.

Stiffman, A.R. 'Physical and Sexual Abuse in Runaway Youths' in *Child Abuse and Neglect,* volume 13, pages 417-426, 1984.

Whitbeck, L.B. and Simons 'Life on the streets - the victimisation of runaway and homeless adolescents' in *Youth and Society,* volume 22 (1), pages 108-125, 1990.